THE OFFICIAL MTO
BUS HANDBOOK

This handbook is only a guide. For official purposes, please refer to the *Ontario Highway Traffic Act* and regulations as well as the *Public Vehicles Act* and regulations.

For more information about driver licensing, visit www.mto.gov.on.ca.

To request a copy of this book in an alternate format, contact Publications Ontario at 1-800-668-9938 or (416) 326-5300 or visit www.publications.serviceontario.ca.

Disponible en français
Demandez le « Guide officiel des autobus publié par le MTO »

DRIVING IS A PRIVILEGE–NOT A RIGHT

INTRODUCTION

The *Official MTO Bus Handbook* is designed to help drivers who want to apply for licences to operate buses, school buses and ambulances. These are classes B, C, E or F driver's licences.

As well as the rules of the road, bus and ambulance drivers need to know the laws governing the operation of vehicles that transport passengers. They must have special driving skills and demonstrate the safe driving practices that apply to those vehicles.

This handbook sets out the information you will need to know and the skills you will be expected to demonstrate in order to qualify for these licences. Some improvements you may notice include a new chapter called The Road Test, plus expanded information on backing and driving in roundabouts.

An applicant for a bus driver's licence is also required to successfully complete a knowledge test for a Class D truck licence. A driver will maintain a Class D licence if temporarily downgraded. In addition to the bus handbook, the driver should study the *Official MTO Truck Handbook*; both should be used together.

This handbook is intended to help a person obtain a commercial class of licence. Effective July 1, 2017 an applicant for a bus driver's licence will take a newly updated road and knowledge test. Many people use a commercial class of driver licence as a way to earn income. The information in this book does not provide enough information about the regulations and compliance requirements necessary to prepare a person to drive commercial vehicles professionally.

A person interested in a career that involves driving commercial vehicles should obtain training by enrolling at a properly certified and accredited driver-training institution.

Drive safely

CONTENTS

CONTENTS

CHAPTER 1
GETTING YOUR LICENCE

I. LEGISLATION

These Acts and regulations govern certain aspects of the movement of passengers and goods, and the operation of vehicles.

1. The *Highway Traffic Act (HTA)* and the following regulations govern the driver, the vehicle and equipment, weight and numbers of passengers that a bus driver can carry: Commercial Motor Vehicle Inspections Reg. 199/07; Commercial Motor Vehicle Operators' Information Reg. 424/97; Covering of Loads R.R.O.1990. Reg.577; Critical Defects of Commercial Motor Vehicles O.Reg.512/97; Equipment R.R.O.1990. Reg.587; Hours of Service O.Reg.555/06; Safety Inspections R.R.O.1990.Reg.611; Security of Loads O.Reg.363/04; School Buses R.R.O.1990.Reg.612.

2. The *Public Vehicles Act* and regulations control the for-hire movement of people on the highways by bus.

II. LICENCE CLASSES AND COMBINATIONS

The Driver's Licence Classification Chart on pages 10 and 11 shows you what class of licence you need to drive different vehicles.

A driver may hold a class A, B, C, D, E, F, G, G1, G2, M, M with L condition, M1, M2, or M2 with L condition driver's licence, or combination. A full class G licence is required to apply for a Class A, B, C, D, E or F licence. A novice driver may not hold a classified licence or a driving instructor's licence.

There are several possible combinations of licences. For example, you can hold a class A and B if you meet the requirements for both. Your licence designation in this case would be shown as AB.

DRIVER'S LICENCE CLASSIFICATION CHART

Class of License		Types of vehicles allowed	May also drive vehicles in class
A		Any tractor-trailer combination	D and G
B		Any school-purposes bus	C, D, E, F and G
C		Any regular bus	D, F and G
D		A motor vehicle exceeding 11,000 kilograms gross weight or registered gross weight or any truck or combination provided the towed vehicle is not over 4,600 kilograms	G
E		School-purposes bus – maximum of 24-passenger capacity	F and G
F		Regular bus – maximum of 24-passenger capacity – and ambulances	G

Diagram 1-1a

Class of License	Types of vehicles allowed
G **G1** **G2**	Allowed to drive any car, van or small truck or combination of vehicle and towed vehicle up to 11,000 kilograms, provided the towed vehicle is not over 4,600 kilograms. A pickup truck towing a house trailer exceeds 4,600 kilograms but the total combined weight of the truck and trailer does not exceed 11,000 kilograms is deemed a Class G.
	Level One of graduated licensing. Holders may drive Class G vehicles with an accompanying fully licensed driver with at least four years' driving experience. Subject to certain conditions.
	Level Two of graduated licensing. Holders may drive Class G vehicles without accompanying driver but are subject to certain conditions.
M **M1** **M2**	Allowed to drive any motorcycles, including motor tricycles, limited-speed motorcycles (motor scooters) and motor-assisted bicycles (mopeds). Holders may also drive a Class G vehicle under the conditions that apply to a Class G1 licence holder.
	Level One of graduated licensing for motorcycles, including motor tricycles, limited-speed motorcycles (motor scooters) and motor-assisted bicycles (mopeds). Holders may drive a motorcycle under certain conditions.
	Level Two of graduated licensing for motorcycles, including motor tricycles, limited-speed motorcycles (motor scooters) and motor-assisted bicycles (mopeds). Holders may drive a motorcycle but only with a zero blood-alcohol level. Holders may also drive a Class G vehicle under the conditions that apply to a Class G1 licence holder.
M with L condition	Holders may operate a limited-speed motorcycle or moped only.
M2 with L condition	Holders may operate a limited-speed motorcycle or moped only.
M with M condition	Holders may operate a motor tricycle only.
M2 with M condition	Holders may operate a motor tricycle only.

Diagram 1-1b

Note: A "Z" air brake endorsement is required on a driver's licence to operate any air brake equipped motor vehicle.

Any class or combination of licence classes from G to A may be combined with a class M licence authorizing the operation of motorcycles if you meet the requirements for class M. The combinations AM, EM, ABM and so on are other examples of combinations.

Medical requirements for classified licences

When applying for a class A, B, C, D, E or F licence, you must provide a completed ministry medical certificate. You can get blank medical forms from any DriveTest Centre in Ontario. A licence will be refused if your physical or medical condition does not meet the standards outlined in the regulations of the *Highway Traffic Act*.

Drivers under the age of 46 must submit a medical report every **five** years. Drivers aged 46 to 64 must submit a medical report every **three** years. Drivers aged 65

and older are required to submit a medical report every year.

If your licence is conditional on wearing corrective lenses, do not drive without wearing them. Your medical practitioner or optometrist is required by law to report to the licensing authorities any health problems that might affect your safe operation of a motor vehicle.

Chapter 1, section II-Summary
By the end of this section, you should know:
- The different licence classifications and what they permit you to drive
- The medical requirements you must meet to maintain a bus driver's licence

III. BUS LICENCE CLASSES C AND F

A class C licence is needed to drive any bus with seats for more than 24 passengers, but not a school-purposes bus carrying passengers. It allows the driver to operate vehicles included in classes D, F and G, but not motorcycles.

A class F licence is needed to drive an ambulance or any bus with seats for 10 or more passengers, but not more than 24 passengers, and not a school-purposes bus carrying passengers. It also allows the driver to operate vehicles included in class G, but not motorcycles.

Note: If you plan to operate a bus equipped with air brakes, you will need a Z endorsement on your licence. Please refer to the *Official MTO Air Brake Handbook* for more information.

Definitions

Here are definitions of some words used in this section.

- **Highway:** a common and public highway, street, avenue, parkway, driveway, square, place, bridge, viaduct or trestle, any part of which is used by the public for the passage of vehicles, including the shoulders of the road and the land between property lines.
- **Roadway:** the part of the highway that is designed or ordinarily used for traffic, not including the shoulder. Where a highway includes two or more separate roadways, the term roadway refers to any one roadway and not all of the roadways together.
- **Bus:** a motor vehicle designed for carrying 10 or more passengers and used for the transportation of persons.

An applicant for a class C or F driver's licence must:

- Be at least 18 years of age
- Hold a valid Ontario class G or higher licence or equivalent issued in a province or territory of Canada
- Meet medical and vision standards
- Have knowledge of bus equipment maintenance and passenger safety and control
- Pass an MTO driver examination or obtain a certificate of competence from a recognized authority by passing a vision screening, knowledge test and driving test in a vehicle of appropriate size

How to obtain a class C or F driver's licence

1. Pick up the necessary forms from any DriveTest Centre in Ontario, including the medical examination report and study material.
2. Take the medical report to a physician of your choice. When the medical report has been completed, return it to the DriveTest Centre selected for your test. Only applicants with satisfactory medical reports may take a knowledge test for a classified licence.
3. You will be required to pass the following tests:
   - A vision screening
   - A knowledge test including traffic signs recognition and operating knowledge of a bus or ambulance
   - An on-road test in a vehicle with an appropriate size

Vision and knowledge test checklist, classes C and F

Before taking the class C or F knowledge test, make sure you have studied the *Official MTO Bus Handbook*.

Bring the following items to the test:
- Two pieces of identification or Ontario driver's licence
- Complete medical report form
- Money for test fees–cash, debit or credit card
- Glasses or contact lenses (if you need to wear them to read or write)

Road test, classes C and F
During your road test
- You will be asked to demonstrate a daily inspection.You will name the item of equipment checked and briefly describe its condition.
- You will be required to drive in traffic and handle the vehicle safely according to the class of licence for which you are applying.
- You will be required to reverse the vehicle into a parking bay or marked area.

Road test checklist, classes C and F
Bring the following items to the road test:
- Appropriate vehicle in good working order
- Glasses (if you need to wear them to drive)
- Wheel chocks or blocks, if the vehicle is equipped with air brakes

Arrive at least 30 minutes before your road-test appointment. All road tests have a set time frame. Before you begin your test, the examiner will inform you of the amount of time you have to complete it.

INSPECTIONS, CLASSES C AND F
Annual and semi-annual inspections
Operators are responsible for having each of their vehicles inspected annually and semi-annually by a licensed motor-vehicle inspection mechanic. The mechanic checks to ensure that the bus is in compliance with all maintenance requirements and component performance standards detailed in the applicable regulations and schedules of the *Highway Traffic Act*.

If the bus is in compliance with all requirements, the mechanic or another person authorized by the inspection station completes an annual or semi-annual inspection certificate and inspection record. These documents come with a corresponding annual (yellow) or semi-annual (orange) inspection sticker (decal), which indicates the month and year of the inspection. The mechanic or other authorized person places the decal on the outside lower right corner of the windshield or right side of the bus as close to the front as possible.

Daily inspection

A driver is not permitted to drive a bus, motor coach, school bus or a school-purposes vehicle unless the driver or another person has, within the previous 24 hours, conducted an inspection of the vehicle and completed an inspection report. The driver must continue to check all systems throughout the day for defects, because the condition of the vehicle can change. The driver and operator are both responsible for the safe operating condition of the commercial motor vehicle. By staying alert, you can spot trouble before it causes a breakdown or collision.

For the full inspection schedules outlining all major and minor defects, which all commercial vehicle drivers are required to complete daily, refer to the Ontario Regulation

199/07 "Commercial Motor Vehicle Inspections" in the *Highway Traffic Act* at www.e-laws. gov.on.ca.

The inspection is conducted in accordance with an inspection schedule. It provides a list of vehicle systems and components that the driver is required to inspect, and provides a list of defects to guide and assist the driver.

The schedule for the inspection depends upon the type of bus and its use, as follows:

Schedule 2

Buses (except school buses), motor coaches, trailers towed by either vehicle.

The inspection schedule divides defects into two categories, major and minor. When a minor defect is identified, the driver must record the defect on the inspection report and report it to the operator. Drivers are not permitted to drive a vehicle with a major defect.

Drivers must carry both the current inspection report and the applicable inspection schedule. Electronic reports and schedules are permitted.

Schedules 3 and 4 for motor coaches

Motor-coach operators have a second inspection process available to them.

The requirements allow the operator to select either the regular bus-inspection process using Schedule 2, as described above, which requires the driver to verify there are no under-vehicle defects, or inspect the bus using a two-stage inspection process.

Under the two-stage process, the driver conducts an inspection of the coach using Schedule 3. A Schedule 3 inspection is similar to that of a Schedule 2 but omits the under-vehicle inspection requirements for the driver. The Schedule 3 inspection is also valid for 24 hours. As with a Schedule 2 inspection, the driver is required to examine and observe the condition of the vehicle during the day or trip.

A Schedule 3 inspection is only valid when the coach has also had a Schedule 4 inspection. A Schedule 4 inspection is conducted by a coach technician and beginning July 1, 2018, is valid for 30 days or 12,000 kilometres, whichever comes last. It consists of a detailed under-vehicle inspection and must be kept in the vehicle.

Outside inspection
- Headlights (low and high beams), turn signals, parking and clearance lights
- Windshield and wipers
- Engine compartment: fluid levels, wiring, belts, hoses and hydraulic brake-fluid leaks (if so equipped)
- Tires
- Wheels, hubs and fasteners
- Exhaust system (check for leaks)
- Stop, tail and hazard lights
- Emergency exits
- Entrance door

- Body condition and frame
- Fuel system (tank, cap and check for leaks)
- Coupling devices, if applicable
- Cargo securement
- Dangerous goods, if present
- Suspension system
- Air brakes for audible air leaks and push rod travel
- Inspection stickers

Inside inspection
- Steering wheel (for excessive freeplay)
- Brake pedal reserve and fade
- Brake booster operation
- Brake-failure warning light
- Parking brake operation
- Brake air-pressure or vacuum gauge
- Warning signal, low air-pressure/vacuum gauge
- Turn indicator and hazard lights, switch and pilot
- Interior lights

- Windshield washer and wipers
- Windshield and windows
- Mirrors, adjustment and condition
- Defroster and heaters
- Horn
- Driver's seat belt and seat security
- Emergency equipment
- Emergency exits
- Driver controls (accelerator pedal, clutch and required gauges)
- Passenger compartment (stanchion padding, damaged steps or floor, damaged or insecure overhead luggage rack or compartment)
- Check accessibility/mobility devices and safety restraints, if applicable

Note: If the vehicle (other than a motor coach) is being used as a school-purposes vehicle, the daily inspection used will be the one on pages 22 to 25.

The daily road check (while driving the vehicle)

Drivers are required to examine and observe the condition of the vehicle during the day or trip. Plan a road check to evaluate your vehicle's steering, suspension, clutch, transmission, driveline and other components. It will help determine whether the engine performs properly, and whether the brakes have enough stopping power. You can do a road check on the way to pick up the first passengers of the day.

Engine check

Be alert for any unusual engine noises, vibrations or lack of normal responses.

Test parking brake

To check this brake, put the vehicle in gear while the parking brake is on. The brake should be able to hold the bus stationary with the transmission in gear and the engine at idle speed.

Note: Driving with the parking brake on is the most frequent cause of parking brake failure.

Check transmission

A manual transmission should allow for smooth, easy gear changes.

Standard transmission-check clutch

When starting an engine, the clutch pedal should be depressed to relieve the starter of the extra load of turning the transmission gears. The clutch should engage easily and smoothly without jerking, slipping excessively or chattering. Never "ride" the clutch pedal. A properly adjusted clutch pedal should have some free play when the pedal is fully released.

While changing gears, carefully control the speed of the engine to shift without jerking or excessive clutch slippage. Erratic or careless gear shifting wears out the clutch.

Check tires and wheels

Another important component of vehicle safety are tires and wheels. You must check the tires and wheels of your vehicle as part of the pre-trip inspection to ensure that they meet safety standards. For example, you must check your tires for appropriate tread depth and your wheels to make sure they are securely attached.

It is also a good safety practice to inspect the wheels, wheel fasteners and tires after having new tires or wheels installed. Wheel manufacturers recommend having fasteners rechecked between 80 and 160 km after installation.

Wheels and tires must be installed by a certified tire installer or a mechanic.

Check the brakes

Test your brakes at low speeds, bringing the vehicle to a complete stop in a straight line. There should be no pulling to one side or excessive noise. Note any extra pedal pressure needed, or sponginess of the pedal. Ensure brakes on the vehicle are not out-of-adjustment at all times. Do not drive the vehicle until problems have been repaired. If your vehicle is equipped with air brakes, please refer to the *Official MTO Air Brake Handbook*.

Check the steering

Free play or lash in the steering system is the distance that the steering wheel moves before the tires begin turning. Check with the engine on and the wheels straight ahead; turn the steering wheel in both directions with your fingers until you can feel the resistance of the tires. If the steering wheel rotates too far, there is excessive free play or lash in the steering system.

Power steering should be quiet, and the vehicle should steer easily in turns or when going over bumps. Look for unusual ride or handling.

Check the suspension

Broken springs, ruptured air bags and faulty shock absorbers may cause sag, bouncing, bottoming and excessive sway when driving.

Stay alert to the condition of your vehicle

Drivers should quickly sense the "thump-thumping" of a flat tire, or one that is underinflated. Keep the right air pressure in the tires at all times to prevent premature tire wear, failure and breakdown. The air pressure in your spare tire should be the same as the pressure in the tire on the vehicle carrying the highest pressure. Again, recognize unusual noises or handling. A vehicle should not be driven with any of these defects.

A police officer or appointed ministry officer has the authority to perform a safety inspection at any time and any location.

Chapter 1, section III-Summary
By the end of this section, you should know:
- The qualifications and requirements for a class C or F licence
- How to obtain a class C or F licence
- How to perform the daily road check

IV. SCHOOL BUS LICENCE CLASSES B AND E

A class B licence is needed to drive any school-purposes bus having seats for more than 24 passengers. It also allows you to operate vehicles included in classes C, D, E, F and G, but not motorcycles.

A class E licence is needed to drive any school-purposes bus having seats for not more than 24 passengers. It also allows you to operate vehicles included in classes F and G, but not motorcycles.

Definitions

Here are definitions of some words used in this section.

- **A bus:** a motor vehicle designed for carrying 10 or more passengers and used for the transportation of people
- **A school-purposes bus is:** a school bus, as defined in subsection 175 (1) of the *Highway Traffic Act*; or a bus while being operated by or under contract with a school board or other authority in charge of a school for the transportation of adults with developmental disabilities or children.
- **A school bus:** is painted chrome yellow, and displays on the front and rear the words "School Bus" and on the rear the words "Do not pass when signals flashing."
- **A school-purposes vehicle is:** a van or station wagon, while being operated by or under a contract with a school board or other authority in charge of a school, for the transportation of six or more adults with a developmental disability, six or more children or six or more persons from both categories.
- **Median strip:** a median is a physical barrier such as a raised, lowered, earth, or paved strip constructed to separate traffic travelling in different directions. Vehicles cannot cross over a median strip.
- **Highway:** a common and public highway, street, avenue, parkway, driveway, square, place, bridge, viaduct or trestle, any part of which is used by the public for the passage of vehicles, including the shoulders of the road and the land between property lines.
- **Roadway:** the part of the highway that is improved, designed or ordinarily used for traffic, not including the shoulder. Where a highway includes two or more separate roadways, the term roadway refers to any one roadway and not all of the roadways together.

Qualification requirements for classes B and E

An applicant for a class B or E driver's licence must:

- Be at least 21 years of age
- Meet medical and vision standards
- Hold a valid Ontario class G or higher licence or equivalent issued in a province or territory of Canada
- Have successfully completed a school-bus driver improvement course approved by MTO and be able to show proof of successful completion with a valid course certificate (valid for five years)
- Have knowledge of bus equipment maintenance and passenger safety and control
- Pass an MTO driver examination or obtain a certificate of competence from a recognized authority by passing a vision screening, knowledge test and a driving test in a bus of appropriate size

- Not have accumulated more than six demerit points on their driving record
- Not have had a driver's licence under suspension at any time within the preceding 12 months as a result of having been convicted or found guilty of:
  - driving under suspension
  - speeding over 50 km above the limit
  - careless driving
  - racing on a highway
  - leaving the scene of an accident
  - a Criminal Code of Canada offence committed by means of a motor vehicle or while driving or having care and control of a motor vehicle
  - flight from police
- Not have been convicted or found guilty within the preceding five years of two or more offences under the Criminal Code of Canada, committed on different dates by means of a motor vehicle, or while driving or having care and control of a motor vehicle
- Not have been convicted or found guilty within the preceding five years under section 4 or 5 of the *Narcotic Control Act* of Canada
- Not have been convicted or found guilty within the preceding five years of certain sexual or moral offences under the Criminal Code of Canada
- Not have been convicted or found guilty of any offence for conduct that affords reasonable grounds for believing that they will not properly perform their duties, or is not a proper person to have custody of children

In addition, a holder of a class B or E driver's licence may not accumulate more than eight demerit points.

How to obtain a class B or E driver's licence

1. Pick up the necessary forms from any DriveTest Centre in Ontario, including the medical-examination report form and study material.
2. Take the medical report to a physician of your choice. When the medical examination has been completed, return the report to the DriveTest Centre selected for your tests. Only applicants with satisfactory medical reports may take a knowledge test for a classified licence.
3. A criminal-record search will be initiated when you pay your application fee.
4. You are required to pass the following:
   - Vision screening
   - Knowledge test including a traffic-signs recognition component and a test of operating knowledge of a school bus
   - Driving test in a vehicle of appropriate seating capacity
   - A satisfactory driver record search
5. Successfully complete a ministry-approved school-bus driver improvement course and obtain a certificate, which is valid for five years.

Vision and knowledge test checklist, classes B and E

Before taking the class B or E knowledge test, make sure you have studied the *Official MTO Bus Handbook*. Bring the following items to the test:
- Two pieces of identification or Ontario driver's licence
- Complete medical report form
- Money for test fees–cash, debit or credit card
- Glasses or contact lenses (if you need to wear them to read or write)

Road test, classes B and E

On your class B or E road test:
- You will demonstrate a daily inspection. You will name the item of equipment checked and briefly describe its condition.
- You will drive in traffic and handle the vehicle safely according to the class of licence for which you are applying.
- You will demonstrate loading and unloading.
- You will be required to reverse the vehicle into a parking bay or marked area.
- You will demonstrate proper procedures at all railway crossings.

Road test checklist, classes B and E

Bring the following items to the road test:
- Appropriate vehicle in good working order
- Glasses (if you need to wear them to drive)
- Wheel chocks or blocks, if the vehicle is equipped with air brakes

Arrive at least 30 minutes before your road-test appointment. All road tests have a set time frame. Before you begin your test, the examiner will inform you of the amount of time you have to complete it.

INSPECTIONS, CLASSES B AND E

Annual and semi-annual inspections

Operators are responsible for having each of their vehicles inspected annually and semi-annually by a licensed motor-vehicle inspection mechanic. The mechanic checks to ensure that the bus is in compliance with all maintenance requirements and component performance standards detailed in the applicable regulations and schedules of the *Highway Traffic Act*.

If the bus is in compliance with all requirements, the mechanic or another person authorized by the inspection station completes an annual or semi-annual inspection certificate and inspection record. These documents come with a corresponding annual or semi-annual inspection sticker (decal), which indicates the month and year of the inspection. The mechanic or other authorized person places the decal on the outside lower right corner of the windshield or right side of the bus as close to the front as possible.

Daily inspection

A driver is not permitted to drive a bus, motor coach, school bus, or, a school-purposes vehicle unless the driver or another person has, within the previous 24 hours, conducted an inspection of the vehicle and completed an inspection report. The driver must continue to check all systems throughout the day for defects, because the condition of the vehicle can change. Both the driver and operator are responsible for the safe operating condition of the commercial motor vehicle. By staying alert, you can spot trouble before it causes a breakdown or collision.

The inspection is conducted in accordance with an inspection schedule. It provides a list of vehicle systems and components that the driver is required to inspect, and provides a list of defects to guide and assist the driver. The schedule for the inspection depends upon the type of bus and its use, as follows:

Schedule 2: trailers towed by school-purposes buses.

Schedule 5: yellow school buses, school-purposes buses.

The inspection schedule divides defects into two categories: major and minor. A major defect such as a flat tire and broken main leaf spring poses immediate safety risks, while minor defects may be less urgent (for example, broken clearance lamps and a damaged wiper blade). When a defect is identified, the driver must record the defect on the daily inspection report, inform the operator, and monitor the condition. Drivers are not permitted to operate a vehicle with a major defect.

A completed, signed daily inspection report is required even when no defect is found. Drivers must carry both the current inspection report and the applicable inspec-

tion schedule at all times. Electronic reports and schedules are permitted.

For the full inspection schedules outlining all major and minor defects, which all commercial vehicle drivers are required to complete daily, refer to the Ontario Regulation 199/07 "Commercial Motor Vehicle Inspections" in the *Highway Traffic Act* at www.e-laws.gov.on.ca. For additional information on how to perform a daily inspection in accordance with Regulation 199/07, go to www.ontario.ca and type the following information into the search box: "Trucks and Buses, Commercial Vehicle Operators' Safety Manual". On the Trucks and Buses page, type "Module 8" in the search box.

Outside inspection
- Alternating lights, front
- Headlights (low and high beams) directional signals, parking and clearance lights

- Windshield and wipers
- Engine compartment: fluid levels, wiring, belts, hoses and hydraulic brake-fluid leaks (if so equipped)
- Tires (retreads on rear wheels only)
- Wheel nuts, hubs and fasteners
- Exhaust system for leaks
- Directional, stop tail and clearance lights
- Emergency exit
- Alternating lights, rear
- Entrance door
- Body condition and frame
- Fuel system (tank, cap, and for leaks)
- Signs (for cleanliness and legibility)
- Stop arm and pedestrian student safety crossing arm
- Coupling devices, if applicable
- Cargo securement
- Dangerous goods, if present
- Suspension system
- Air brakes for audible air leaks and push rod travel
- Inspection stickers

Inside inspection

- Steering wheel
  (for excessive freeplay)
- Brake pedal reserve and fade
- Brake booster operation
- Brake-failure warning light
- Parking brake operation
- Brake air-pressure or vacuum gauge
- Warning signal, low-air
  pressure/vacuum
- Interior (for exhaust fumes)
- Signal and hazard lights,
  switch and pilot
- Alternating lights, switch
  and signal device
- Interior lights
- Windshield washer and
  wipers
- Windshield and windows
- Mirrors, adjustment and
  condition
- Defroster and heaters
- Horn
- Stop arm mechanism
- Driver's seat belt and seat security

Diagram 1-2

Diagram 1-3

- Service door and controls
- Passenger's seat security
- Emergency exit and warning signal
- Floor covering (tripping hazards)
- Fire extinguisher
- First-aid kit
- Flares or reflectors
- Interior (for cleanliness)
- Passenger seat belts (if so equipped)
- Driver controls (accelerator pedal, clutch and required gauges)
- Passenger compartment (stanchion padding, damaged steps or floor, damaged or insecure overhead luggage rack or compartment)
- Check accessibility/mobility devices and safety restraints, if applicable

Final check before driving onto the highway:
- Driver's seat belt fastened
- Drive forward and brake to a stop to test the service brake
- Additional check of all gauges– heat, oil and vacuum, etc.
- Complete log-book entry

Note: A bus (other than a motor coach) that has previously been used by the same owner as a school-purposes bus, can be inspected using schedule 5, even on days when the bus is not being used for a school-purposes trip.

The daily road check (while driving the vehicle)

Drivers are required to examine and observe the condition of the vehicle during the day or trip. Plan a road check to evaluate your vehicle's steering, suspension, clutch, transmission, driveline and other components to determine whether the engine performs properly, and whether the brakes have enough stopping power.

You can do a road check on the way to pick up the first passengers of the day.

Check the suspension

Broken springs, ruptured air bags and faulty shock absorbers may cause sag, bouncing, bottoming and excessive sway when under way.

Engine check

Be alert for any unusual engine noises, vibrations or lack of normal responses.

Check the steering

Free play or lash in the steering system is the distance the steering wheel moves before the tires begin turning. Check with the engine on and the wheels straight ahead; turn the steering wheel in both directions with your fingers until you can feel the resistance of the tires. If the steering wheel rotates too far, there is excessive free play or lash in the steering system.

Power steering should be quiet, and the vehicle should steer easily in turns or when going over bumps. Look for unusual ride or handling.

Check transmission and clutch

A manual transmission should allow for smooth, easy gear changes.

The clutch should engage easily and smoothly without jerking, slipping excessively or chattering. Never "ride" the clutch pedal. A properly adjusted clutch pedal should have some free play when the pedal is fully released.

While changing gears, carefully control the speed of the engine to shift without jerking or excessive clutch slippage. Erratic or careless gear shifting wears out the clutch.

Check tires and wheels

Another important component of vehicle safety are tires and wheels. You must check the tires and wheels of your vehicle as part of the pre-trip inspection to ensure that they meet safety standards. For example, you must check your tires for appropriate tread depth and your wheels to make sure they are securely attached.

It is also a good safety practice to inspect the wheels, wheel fasteners and tires after having new tires or wheels installed. Wheel manufacturers recommend having fasteners rechecked between 80 km and 160 km after installation.

Wheels and tires must be installed by a certified tire installer or a mechanic.

Test parking brake
To check this brake, put the vehicle in gear while the parking brake is on. The brake should be able to hold the bus stationary with the transmission in gear and the engine at idle speed.

Check the brakes
Test at low speeds, bringing the vehicle to a complete stop. The vehicle should stop in a straight line. There should be no pulling to one side or excessive noise. Note any extra pedal pressure or sponginess. Ensure at all times that brakes are not out of adjustment. Do not operate the vehicle until such conditions have been repaired.

Note: Driving with the parking brake on is the most frequent cause of parking brake failure.

Stay alert to the condition of your vehicle
Drivers should quickly sense the "thump-thumping" of a flat tire, or one that is underinflated. Keep the right air pressure in the tires to prevent premature tire wear, failure and breakdown. The air pressure in your spare tire should be the same as the pressure in the tire on the vehicle carrying the highest pressure. Again, recognize unusual noises or handling. A vehicle should not be driven with any of these defects.

A police officer or appointed ministry officer has the authority to perform a safety inspection at any time and any location.

Chapter 1, section IV-Summary
By the end of this section, you should know:
- The qualifications and requirements for a class B or E licence
- How to obtain a class B or E licence
- How to perform the daily road check

CHAPTER 2
DRIVING A BUS

Defensive driving

The most important concern for a bus driver is the safety of the passengers. Professional drivers who carry passengers must observe the rules of the road, understand and practice defensive driving, and take special precautions in loading and unloading.

The professional looks ahead, thinks ahead, acts early and drives defensively. A person who drives defensively:

- Keeps adequate space around the vehicle and manages the blind spot
- Keeps his or her eyes moving, and checks traffic as far down the roadway and to the sides
- Checks the mirrors frequently
- Recognizes possible danger far enough in advance to take preventive action
- Makes allowances for the errors of other drivers and pedestrians
- Gives up the right-of-way if it will avoid possible danger to the driver or passengers
- Makes allowances for the rapidly changing conditions of the road, weather and traffic
- Shows courtesy to other road users
- Wears a seat belt
- Uses headlights at all times to make sure the bus is easily seen
- Drives at a safe speed, slowing when road conditions can affect stopping distance or vehicle control

10 WAYS YOU CAN HELP MAKE ONTARIO'S ROADS THE SAFEST IN NORTH AMERICA

1. Don't drink and drive. Don't drive when you're taking medication that will affect your driving.

2. Wear your seat belt (unless you are a passenger on a bus without seat belts).

3. Obey the speed limits. Slow down when road and weather conditions are poor.

4. Don't take risks: don't cut people off in traffic, make sudden lane changes or run yellow lights.

5. Don't drive when you're tired, upset or sick.

6. If you're in doubt, let the other driver go first—yield the right-of-way.

7. Keep a safe distance between your vehicle and the one ahead.

8. Avoid distractions associated with electronic devices such as cell phones and GPS. Never text message while driving, and keep two-way radio conversations to a minimum.

9. Check your mirrors frequently; be aware of blind spots not covered by the mirrors.

10. Check traffic in all directions before going into an intersection.

I. DRIVING TECHNIQUES

Diagram 2-1

Steering (forward) and off-track

The rear wheels of the vehicle do not pivot and so will not follow the same path as the front wheels. In a curve, the greater the distance (wheel base) between the front wheels and the rear wheels of the vehicle, the greater the amount of "off-track." The off-track path of the rear wheels is closer to the curb than the path of the front wheels.

On the highway, you must lead your turning arc of the front wheels according to the sharpness of the curve and your vehicle's off-track.

On a curve to the right, keep the front wheels close to the left side of the lane to prevent dropping the rear wheels off the pavement.

On a curve to the left, keep the front wheels closer to the right edge of the pavement to prevent the rear wheels from crossing into the other traffic lane.

Whenever possible, make turns from the proper lanes. When you must use portions of another lane to make sharp turns, it is your responsibility to be sure that such a move can be made safely, without interfering with other road users (Diagram 2-1).

Right turns

Right turns with vehicles that have a lot of off-track require the driver to lead the turning arc according to the amount of off-track. Running the rear wheels of the vehicle over curbs and sidewalks is dangerous and may cause damage to the suspension, wheels and tires. You must be careful not to hit objects such as power poles, sign posts or lamp standards mounted close to the curb. Generally, it is better to use more space from the road you are entering than from the road you are leaving.

In narrow streets, proceed well into the intersection before turning the steering wheel. You may need to travel partially over the centre line of

Diagram 2-2

the street entered or into the second traffic lane. If so, you must yield to traffic, signal the turn and ensure a safe manoeuvre. When you have to partially block off another lane in

this manner, make sure that smaller vehicles such as motorcycles and bicycles are not moving up on your right side. Remember, your ability to see is restricted when you are in the middle of a turn (Diagram 2-2).

Left turns

Be aware of any off-tracking when making a left turn. Unless you use your left outside mirror to monitor the path of the rear wheels, those wheels may hit a vehicle or a sign post on an island. You must turn the vehicle in a wide arc before bringing it back to its proper position after a left turn, just right of the centre line. Then as you speed up, you can move, when it is safe, to the right lane (see Diagram 2-3 on next page).

Note: School buses, especially larger buses, have their rear axles well ahead of the end of the bus causing the rear of the bus to swing out of its normal path.

Backing

Planning your route in advance may eliminate the need for backing. If necessary, drive around the block if it will help you avoid backing around a corner. Drive out into traffic, rather than backing into traffic. Avoid entering the path of a reversing vehicle, and do not stop or park behind a vehicle that may soon be reversed. As the driver, you are responsible for ensuring all precautions are taken when attempting to back into a driveway from the road.

Diagram 2-3

Straight backing

The easiest and safest backing manoeuvre is straight backing. Whenever possible use this approach.

- Pull ahead and position the bus in line with the direction you want it to take.
- Ensure front and rear wheels are straight and centred.
- Watch both mirrors while backing slowly in a straight line.
- If the bus shifts left or right from the parking spot, align the vehicle accordingly.

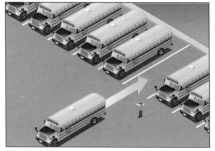

Diagram 2-4

- Prior to backing: Turn off phone/radio, open windows, activate four-way flashers and sound horn.
- Exit the vehicle and walk around to examine the area into which you must back. Look for overhead obstacles or wires, side clearances, pedestrians or objects in your path of travel.
- Remember to use both rearview mirrors. Keep in mind the blind spot on the rear as vision is limited.

Alley dock (driver's side)

When performing an alley dock, backing from the driver's side is recommended.

- Position your bus to the angled direction you want it to take.
- Turn steering wheel to the left while backing slowly.
- Look out driver's window to monitor the rear while checking mirrors.
- If the turn is too early or sharp, turn wheels slightly to the right accordingly. If the turn is too late

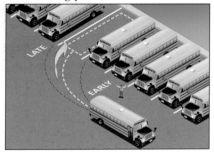

Diagram 2-5

or wide, adjust wheels by turning it to the left.

Offset backing (driver's side)

There are two types of offset backing: driver side, where you offset back to the left; and passenger side, where you offset back to the right.

- Drive straight forward until the vehicle is in a straight line.
- Turn the wheel all the way to the left angling the bus toward the destination.
- Back up while watching the mirrors to frame the destination parking spot.
- Back up the bus until the rear is aligned with the centre of the parking spot.
- Stop and turn the wheel to the right as far as possible and backup until the rear is positioned to enter the parking spot.
- Straighten the wheels. Look out both mirrors while slowly backing toward the destination.

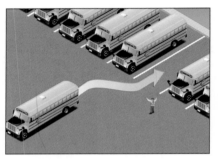

Diagram 2-6

Guide

A responsible guide can help you by watching the area into which you are backing and by keeping an eye on your blind-spot zone. The guide should stand in a position to see you and the area to the rear of your vehicle clearly. They should also be prepared to warn you if pedestrians or vehicles move into your path as you back. This can help you make an easy and safe approach to the dock. Remember that back-up alarm devices do not absolve the driver's responsibility when reversing.

Brake inspection

While you are not expected to be able to repair your brakes, you should be able to tell when there is a problem. Use the following inspection routine as part of your daily trip inspection.

1. Hydraulic brakes (without power assist):
   • Apply brakes moderately and hold.
   • If the pedal shows a steady drop, the vehicle should be taken out of service and the system in spected professionally.
2. Hydraulic brakes (with power assist):
   • With the engine stopped, pump the brake pedal several times to eliminate power assist.
   • Apply brakes moderately and hold.
   • Start the engine (the pedal should drop slightly) and stop.

• If the pedal continues to drop or does not drop (no power assist), stop the engine. The vehicle should be taken out of service and the system inspected professionally.

Use of brakes

Apply brakes with steady pressure at the beginning of a stop, then ease off as the vehicle slows. Just before the vehicle comes to a complete stop, release brakes to avoid jerk and rebound, then brake again to hold the vehicle while stopped.

Hydraulic brakes or air brakes should not be fanned (alternately applied and released) except on slippery pavement where this type of braking may give better control, reduce the danger of skidding and give a shorter stop. However, fanning air brakes may sharply reduce air pressure. Fanning serves no useful purpose on dry pavement and, on a long downhill grade, may reduce air

pressure below the minimum needed for stopping the vehicle.

Avoid excessive use of brakes on long downgrades, because overheated brakes are dangerously inefficient. Gear down to use engine compression as the principal means of controlling speed on long grades. You should use the same gear going down a long grade as you would to climb it. Choose the lower gear before you begin going downhill.

If the low air-pressure warning device operates at any time, stop immediately in the safest available place and have the problem corrected before you proceed.

If your brakes fail on a level road, down-shift (manual or automatic) and use engine compression to slow the vehicle. In an emergency, it may be necessary to use the emergency brake. Do not drive the vehicle again until repairs have been made.

Take care when braking on a wet or slippery surface or on a curve. Late or over-braking in these circumstances could cause skidding. To stop a skid, release the brakes, look and steer in the direction you want to go.

Retarders have become a popular option on motor coaches. They augment braking and help reduce service brake wear and brake fade, and are useful on long downhill grades.

There are three types of brake retarders: exhaust brakes, engine brakes and driveline (transmission) retarders. Activation of the retarder is usually controlled by the driver by means of an "on-off" or variable setting switch. In some buses, the retarder activates automatically when the service brakes are applied. Exhaust and engine brake retarders typically increase engine noise and many communities prohibit their use.

Always respect signs advising against the use of engine or exhaust brakes. Drive line retarders don't increase engine noise. However, prolonged use increases transmission heat to the point that it could shut down the coach to protect the transmission from damage.

Warning: Because the retarder applies brake force only to the drive axle, activating the retarder while driving on a slippery surface can cause a loss of control and a collision. Do not use the retarder on wet, slippery or icy roads. During inclement weather, turn off the retarder using the maters (on-off) switch. Drivers who ignore this warning and experience a retarder-induced wheel lock-up or spin should immediately turn off the retarder to allow the drive wheels to roll freely and regain steering control.

Note: If you plan to operate a vehicle equipped with air brakes, refer to the *Official MTO Air Brake Handbook* for more information.

Following distance

Commercial motor vehicles must keep a minimum distance of at least 60 metres (200 ft.) between themselves and other vehicles when on a highway at a speed over 60 km/h (40 mph), except when overtaking and passing another vehicle.

Stopping at Railway Crossings

All railway crossings on public roads in Ontario are marked with red and white "X" signs. Watch for these signs and be prepared to stop. You may also see yellow advance warning signs and pavement markings of a large X at approaches to railway-crossings. Some railway crossings have flashing signal lights while some use gates or barriers to keep motorists from crossing the tracks when a train is coming.

Most buses and other public vehicles are required to stop at railway crossings that do not have automatic warning devices such as barriers and signal lights. School buses must stop at all railway crossings whether or not they have automatic warning devices. Motorists must be prepared to stop behind these vehicles. Obey all signs and signals. Remember– it can take up to two kilometres for a train to stop under full emergency braking.

When you come to a railway crossing, remember:

- Slow down, listen and look both ways to make sure the way is clear before crossing the tracks.
- If a train is coming, stop at least five metres from the nearest rail. Do not cross the track until you are sure the train or trains have passed.
- Never race a train to a crossing.
- If there are signal lights, wait until they stop flashing and, if the crossing has a gate or barrier, wait until it rises, before you cross the tracks.

- Never drive around, under or through a railway gate or barrier while it is down, being lowered or being raised. It is illegal and dangerous.
- Never stop on railway tracks. For example, in heavy traffic, make sure you have enough room to cross the tracks completely before you begin to cross.
- Don't shift gears while crossing tracks.

- If you get trapped on a crossing, immediately get everyone out and away from the vehicle. Move to a safe place and then contact authorities.
- Buses and other public vehicles are required to stop at railway crossings that are not protected by gates, signal lights, or a stop sign. School buses must stop at railway crossings whether or not they are protected by gates

Diagram 2-7

or signal lights. Watch for these buses and be prepared to stop behind them.

- If you are approaching a railway crossing with a stop sign, you must stop unless otherwise directed by a flagman.

II. SHARING THE ROAD
Sharing the road with smaller vehicles

Be aware that most drivers of smaller vehicles do not understand what it is like to drive a vehicle such as a tractor trailer or bus. Many do not realize that some large vehicles need twice as much stopping distance as the average car, and take much longer to get up to normal driving speed. Many drivers also feel nervous when a large vehicle comes up behind or beside them, and this may cause them to make sudden or unexpected moves.

Here are some tips for sharing the road with smaller vehicles:

1. **Following:** It is very dangerous to follow to closely behind another vehicle. If something unexpected occurs, you will not have enough room to stop safely. Also, be aware that a large vehicle looming up closely behind may intimidate drivers of small vehicles.
2. **Being Passed:** Be courteous when smaller, faster vehicles are trying to pass you. Slow down enough to allow the vehicle to fit in quickly and safely in front of you.
3. **Signalling:** Signal your intentions clearly before turning, slowing or stopping so that other drivers will have adequate time to react appropriately.
4. **Turning:** Many drivers of smaller vehicles do not understand how much room large vehicles need in order to make a turn. Drivers of smaller vehicles will often drive up into the large vehicle's turning space, not

realizing until too late that the large vehicle needs that space to complete the turn. To safely complete a turn, you should proceed slowly and observe the rear of the vehicle. Always check to make sure a vehicle has not moved up into your turning space before completing your turn.

Sharing the road with motorcycles, limited-speed motorcycles or mopeds

Motorcycles, limited-speed motor-cycles and mopeds are harder to see because of their size. Drivers of these vehicles may make sudden moves because of uneven road surfaces or poor weather conditions. Because they are less protected, they are more likely to be injured in a collision.

Motorcycles and mopeds that cannot keep up with traffic should drive as close as possible to the right edge of the road; however, remember that these vehicles have the right to use the whole lane.

Since many motorcycle turn signals do not automatically shut off, be careful when turning left in front of an oncoming motorcycle with its turn signal on. Make sure the motorcyclist is actually turning; he or she may have just forgotten to switch off the turn signal.

Sharing the road with cyclists

Bicycles and mopeds travelling at a lower speed than other traffic are expected to ride about one metre from the curb or parked cars, or as close as practical to the right-hand edge of the road when there is no curb. However, they can use any part of the lane if necessary for safety, such as to:

- Avoid obstacles such as puddles, ice, sand, debris, rutted or grooved pavement, potholes and sewer grates
- Cross railway or streetcar tracks at a 90° angle
- Discourage passing where the lane is too narrow to be shared safely

Cyclists are not required to ride close to the right edge of the road when they are travelling at or faster than the normal speed of traffic at that time and place, or when they are turning left, or getting in position to turn left. (Cyclists are permitted to make a left turn from a left-turn lane, where one is available.)

When passing a cyclist, drivers of motor vehicles are required to maintain a minimum distance of one metre, where practical between their vehicle and the cyclist. Failure to do so may result in a fine in the range of $60 to $500 and an additional two demerit points on the driver's record. Whenever possible, you should change lanes to pass.

Do not follow too closely behind cyclists. They do not have brake lights to warn you when they are slowing or stopping.

Intersections – To avoid collisions with bicyclists at intersections, remember the following:

Diagram 2-8

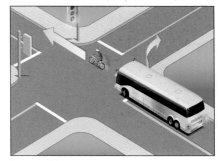

Diagram 2-9

- When turning right, signal and check your mirrors and the blind spot to your right to make sure you do not cut off a cyclist.
- When turning left, you must stop and wait for oncoming bicycles to pass before turning.
- When driving through an intersection, be careful to scan for cyclists waiting to turn left.

Do not sound your horn unnecessarily when you are overtaking a cyclist. It may frighten them and cause them to lose control. If you feel that you must use your horn, tap it quickly and lightly while you are still some distance away from the cyclist.

Bike lanes are reserved for cyclists. They are typically marked by a solid white line. Sometimes you will need to enter or cross a bike lane to turn right at a corner or driveway. Take extra care when you do this. Enter the bike lane only after ensur-

ing that you can do so safely, and then make the turn.

Watch for cyclists' hand signals. A cyclist may indicate a right-hand turn by extending their right arm.

Try to make eye contact when possible with cyclists.

Bike boxes help prevent collisions between motorists and bicycles at intersections. It is typically a painted box on the road with a white bicycle symbol inside. Bicycle lanes approaching and leaving the box may also be painted. As a driver, you must stop for a traffic signal behind the bike box. Do not stop in the box.

Children riding bicycles on the street may lack the necessary training and skills for safe cycling. They may not be aware of all the dangers or the rules of the road. Watch for children on oversized bicycles as they may not have the ability to control it.

When parked on the side of the roadway, look behind you and check

your mirrors and blind spots for a passing cyclist before opening a door.

Sharing the road with farm machinery

Farm machinery moves quite slowly compared to other road users. Most tractors and combines have a maximum speed of 40 km/h, but travel at less than 40 km/h when towing implements or wagons. Farm machinery is often oversized, wide or long or both, making it difficult for the driver to see vehicles coming up from behind. Farmers often turn directly into fields rather than roads or lanes, or move from lane to lane. Remember that it is common for farmers to be on the roads after dark during peak planting and harvesting seasons.

Farm machinery on the road must display an orange and red slow-moving vehicle sign on the rear of the vehicle. The sign warns other drivers that the vehicle is travelling at 40 km/h or less. If you see one of these signs, slow down and be cautious. Stay well back and do not pass until it is safe to do so. (See the slow-moving vehicle sign on page 81.)

Sharing the road with pedestrians

Pay special attention to pedestrians, whether they are crossing roads in traffic, walking or jogging alongside roads, or using crosswalks or crossovers (generally known as crossings). Drivers should be aware of pedestrians who often will jay-walk not just cross at intersections. **Note** that a ball bouncing into the roadway may be followed by a child or animal. Watch for children. Drive slowly and cautiously through school zones, residential areas and any other area where children may be walking or playing. You never know when a child might dart out from between parked cars or try to cross a street without checking for

oncoming traffic. Be very cautious at twilight when children may still be playing outside, but are very difficult to see. Watch out for Community Safety Zone signs as they indicate areas where the community has identified that there is a special risk to pedestrians.

Seniors or pedestrians with disabilities need extra caution and courtesy from drivers, as they may be slow in crossing the road. Be alert for pedestrians who are blind, with a visual or hearing disability, people who use wheelchairs or people walking slowly due to some other physical disabilities. Give them appropriate consideration. Pedestrians who are blind or visually impaired may use a white cane or guide dog to help them travel safely along sidewalks and across intersections. Drivers of hybrid vehicles should be aware that vision impaired persons often rely on hearing the sound of an en-

gine before entering an intersection. Be aware that when you are slowing or stopping, your vehicle makes little or no discernible noise, extra caution is required. Caution signs are posted in some areas where there is a special need for drivers to be alert.

People operating mobility devices (motorized wheelchair and medical scooters) are treated the same way as pedestrians. Usually these operators will travel along a sidewalk but, if there is no sidewalk available, they should travel, like pedestrians, along the left shoulder of the roadway facing oncoming traffic.

Some streetcar stops have a special safety island or zone for passengers getting on and off. Pass these safety islands and zones at a reasonable speed. Always be ready in case pedestrians make sudden or unexpected moves.

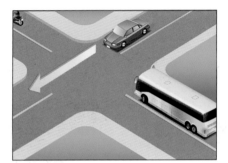

Diagram 2-10

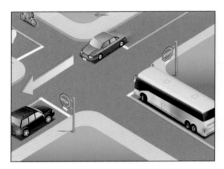

Diagram 2-11

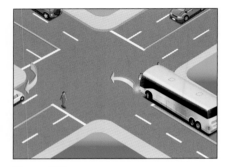

Diagram 2-12

Yielding the right-of-way

There are times when you must yield the right-of-way. This means you must let another person go first. Here are some rules about when you must yield the right-of-way:

At an intersection without signs or lights, you must yield the right-of-way to any vehicle approaching from the right (Diagram 2-10).

At an intersection with stop signs at all corners, you must yield the right-of-way to the first vehicle to come to a complete stop. If two vehicles stop at the same time, the vehicle on the left must yield to the vehicle on the right (Diagram 2-11).

At any intersection where you want to turn left or right, you must yield the right-of-way. If you are turning left, you must wait for approaching traffic to pass or turn and for pedestrians in your path to cross. If you are turning right, you must wait for pedestrians to cross (Diagram 2-12).

A yield sign means you must slow down or stop if necessary and yield the right-of-way to traffic in the intersection or on the intersecting road.

When entering a road from a private road or driveway, you must yield to vehicles on the road and pedestrians on the sidewalk (Diagram 2-13).

You must yield the right-of-way and remain stopped for pedestrians to completely cross the road at

Diagram 2-13

Diagram 2-14

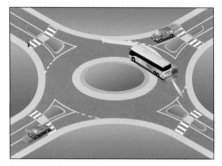

Diagram 2-15

specially marked pedestrian crossings or crossovers (Diagram 2-14), as well as school crossings with crossing guards.

Remember, signalling does not give you the right-of-way. You must make sure the way is clear.

Driving in roundabouts

Allow extra room alongside large vehicles (trucks and buses). They may have to swing wide on the approach or within the roundabout.

Driving a large vehicle in a roundabout

A driver negotiating a roundabout in a large vehicle (such as a truck or bus) may need to use the full width of the roadway, including the central apron (a mountable portion of the centre island adjacent to the roadway), if provided. Prior to entering the roundabout, the vehicle may need to occupy both lanes. Remember, the vehicle in the roundabout has right-

of-way. You must ensure your vehicle is in the appropriate lane for both entry and exit.

Many roundabouts are also designed with a central apron, a raised section of pavement around the central island that acts as an extra lane for large vehicles. The back wheels of the oversized vehicle can ride up on the central apron so that the vehicle can easily complete the turn, while the raised portion of concrete discourages use by smaller vehicles.

Municipal bus bays

Many municipal roadways have special indented stopping areas for municipal buses, called bus bays, where passengers can get on and off. There are three types of bus bays:

- Mid-block indented bays
- Indentations immediately before and after intersections
- Bus-stop areas between two designated parking areas (Diagram 2-16).

When a bus in a bus bay begins flashing its left-turn signals, indicating that it is ready to leave the bus bay, and you are approaching in the lane adjacent to the bus bay, you must allow the bus to re-enter traffic.

If you are a bus driver re-entering traffic from a bus bay, flash your left turn signals to indicate that you are ready to leave the bus bay.

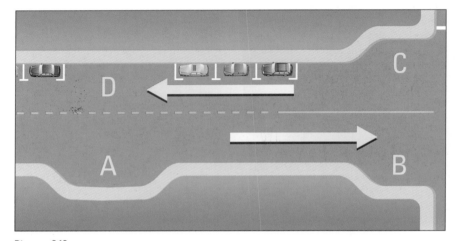

Diagram 2-16

This tells other drivers who are approaching in the lane adjacent to the bus bay that you are going to re-enter traffic. Proceed with caution.

A   Mid-block indented bays
B   An indentation before an intersection
C   An indentation after an intersection
D   Bus stops between legally parked cars

III. HOURS OF SERVICE

This section provides an overview of the basic rules. All the details of the hours-of-service requirements are contained in the *Highway Traffic Act* in Ontario Regulation 555/06.

The hours-of-service regulations apply to drivers of the following types of vehicles:
- Commercial motor vehicles having gross weight or registered gross weight over 4,500 kilograms
- Buses, school buses and school-purposes buses

Exemptions to hours-of-service regulations

Drivers of the following types of vehicles are not required to comply with the hours-of-service regulations:
- Commercial motor vehicles, other than buses, having gross weight or registered gross weight of not more than 4,500 kilograms
- Commercial motor vehicles leased for no longer than 30 days by an individual
- Commercial motor vehicles, operated under dealer or service permits, that are not transporting passengers or goods
- Commercial motor vehicles operated under the authority of In-Transit permits
- Two- or three-axle commercial motor vehicles transporting primary farm, forest, sea or lake products
- Pick-up trucks, being used for personal purposes, which have a manufacturer's gross vehicle weight rating of 6,000 kilograms or less
- Tow trucks
- Motor homes
- Municipal buses operated as part of a public transit service
- Buses used for personal purposes without compensation
- Vehicles being used by a police officers
- Cardiac-arrest vehicles
- Vehicles engaged in providing relief in emergencies
- Ambulances, fire apparatus, hearses or casket wagons

Duty status

The rules define four categories of duty time for commercial vehicle drivers:
- Off-duty time, other than time spent in a sleeper berth

- Off-duty time spent in a sleeper berth
- On-duty time spent driving
- On-duty time, other than time spent driving

On-duty activities include driving, as well as performing any other activities for the operator, such as: inspecting, cleaning or repairing your vehicle; travelling as a co-driver (not including when in sleeper berth); loading and unloading the vehicle; waiting at inspections for unloading or loading to be completed; or because of an unforeseen occurrence such as an accident.

These four categories are used to determine the minimum off-duty hours required and the maximum on-duty hours allowed for commercial vehicle drivers.

Hours-of-service requirements
1. Daily requirement*
- A driver must have 10 hours off-duty in a day.
- A driver cannot drive more than 13 hours in a day.
- A driver cannot drive after 14 hours on-duty in a day.

Some exceptions apply; refer to Ontario Regulation 555/06.

2. Mandatory off-duty time
- After a period of at least eight hours off-duty, a driver cannot drive more than 13 hours.
- After a period of at least eight hours off-duty, a driver cannot drive after having been on-duty for 14 hours.
- After a period of at least eight hours off-duty, a driver cannot drive after 16 hours has elapsed.

3. Cycle requirement
- An operator shall designate a cycle for the driver to follow.
- There are two cycles available, a seven-day cycle or a 14-day cycle.
- In a period of seven consecutive days, a driver cannot drive after having been on-duty for 70 hours.
- In a period of 14 consecutive days, a driver cannot drive after having been on-duty for 120 hours. Drivers following this cycle shall not drive after accumulating 70 hours on-duty without having taken 24 consecutive hours of off-duty time.
- On any day, all drivers must have a period of at least 24 consecutive hours off-duty in the preceding 14 days.

4. Cycle reset/switching
- A driver may only switch the cycle they are on if they start a new cycle.
- To start a new cycle, a driver on the seven-day cycle must take 36 consecutive hours off-duty.
- To start a new cycle, a driver on the 14-day cycle must take 72 consecutive hours off-duty.

5. Daily log requirement
A daily log may be handwritten, computer-generated or made by

means of a recording device. The daily log must contain the following information:

- The driver's name
- The date
- The name of the driver's co-drivers, if any
- The start time of the day being recorded, if the day does not start at midnight
- The cycle that the driver is following
- The odometer reading at the start of the day
- The number plate of each commercial motor vehicle to be driven and each trailer
- The name of the operator
- The address of the driver's home terminal and of the principal place of business of the operator
- Graph grid as illustrated in Form 1 of the regulation (not required for Recording Device)

- The start and end times for each duty status during the day
- The location where the driver's duty status changes
- The total time spent in each duty status during the day
- The odometer reading at the end of the day
- The total distance driven by the driver
- The driver's signature

Daily log exemption

A driver is not required to keep a daily log if the driver:

1. Drives the commercial motor vehicle solely within a radius of 160 kilometres of the location at which the driver starts the day
2. Returns at the end of the day to the same location from which he or she started
3. Only works for one operator that day

If a driver is not required to keep a daily log, the operator shall keep a record for the day showing:

- The date, driver's name and the location where the driver starts and ends the day
- The cycle that the driver is following
- The hour at which each duty status starts and ends
- The total number of hours spent in each duty status

These rules will help keep Ontario's roads safe by allowing commercial drivers to get the rest they need in order to safely operate their vehicles. For more details about the hours-of-service requirements, visit the MTO website at www.mto.gov.on.ca, or refer to the *Highway Traffic Act* at www.e-laws.gov.on.ca.

Chapter 2-Summary

By the end of this chapter, you should know:

- The concept of defensive driving
- How to steer in forward, reverse and while turning
- The meaning of "off-track" and where to position your vehicle on the road
- The importance of sharing the road with other road users especially small vehicles, farm machinery, cyclists and pedestrians
- The concept of right-of-way and common situations where you must yield to other road users
- The rules for hours of service
- How and when to back up; straight backing; how to perform an alley dock from the driver's side; and offset backing from the driver's side.

CHAPTER 3
SAFE AND RESPONSIBLE DRIVING

Driving a bus is a specialized skill that requires you to be alert to what is happening on the inside and outside of the vehicle. Here are some items to keep in mind before you start out:

Special precautions

- Starting and stopping a vehicle should be a smooth, gradual operation. With a manual (standard) transmission, use the hand brake to hold the vehicle while co-ordinating the clutch and accelerator. This helps prevent rolling back on an upgrade. Thinking ahead can eliminate the need for sudden stops.
- Bad weather requires all drivers to adjust their driving habits and take extra care. Noise, worries and other distractions slow down a driver's ability to react. Slow down and keep more clear space around the vehicle. A vehicle with manual transmission and conventional tires may start a great deal easier on icy roads if you place the gear selector lever in second gear.

- Think ahead, and prepare for hazards such as narrow or rough roads, sharp turns, narrow bridges and severe dust by slowing down.
- Ventilate and heat the vehicle when necessary.
- Close and secure all doors when the vehicle is moving.
- Never permit an unauthorized person to sit in the driver's seat, operate the vehicle or any of its controls.
- Do not allow passengers to obstruct the vision of the driver to the front, sides or rear.
- Never load the vehicle beyond its licensed capacity. (This does not apply to city buses, which are allowed to operate over seated capacity with no limit on standees.)
- Except when passing, keep 60 metres (200 ft.) between buses travelling in the same direction on a highway outside a city, town or village.

I. DRIVING AT NIGHT AND IN BAD WEATHER

At night and in weather conditions such as rain, snow or fog, you cannot see as far ahead, even with headlights. Slow down when driving at night, especially on unlit roads and whenever weather conditions reduce your visibility.

Overdriving your headlights

You are overdriving your headlights when your stopping distance is farther than you can see with your headlights. This is a dangerous thing to do because you may not give yourself enough room to make a safe stop. Reflective road signs can mislead you as well, making you believe you can see farther than you really can. This may cause you to overdrive your headlights if you are not careful.

Glare

Glare is dazzling light that makes it hard for you to see and be aware of what others around you are doing.

It can be a problem on both sunny and overcast days, depending on the angle of the sun's rays and your surroundings. Glare can also be a problem at night when you face bright headlights or see them reflected in your mirrors.

When meeting oncoming vehicles with bright headlights at night, look up and beyond and slightly to the right of the oncoming lights. In daytime glare, use your sun visor or use a pair of good-quality sunglasses. When you enter a tunnel on a bright day, slow down to let your eyes adjust to the reduced light. Remove your sunglasses and turn on your headlights when driving through a tunnel.

Cut down glare at night by following the rules of the road for vehicle lights. Use your low-beam headlights within 150 metres (500 ft.) of an oncoming vehicle or when following a vehicle within 60 metres (200 ft.). On country roads, switch to low beams when you come to a curve or hilltop so you can see oncoming headlights and won't blind oncoming drivers. If you can't see any headlights, switch back to high beams.

Fog

Fog is a thin layer of cloud resting on the ground. Fog reduces visibility for drivers, resulting in difficult driving conditions. The best thing to do is to avoid driving in fog. Check weather forecasts and if there is a fog warning, delay your trip until it clears. If that is not possible or if you get caught driving in fog, there are a number of safe driving tips you should follow. If visibility is decreasing rapidly, move off the road and into a safe parking area to wait for the fog to lift.

TIPS FOR DRIVING SAFELY IN FOG

Before you drive—and during your trip—check weather forecasts. If there is a fog warning, delay your trip until it clears. It could save your life. If you are caught driving in fog, follow these safe-driving tips:

DO

- Slow down gradually and drive at a speed that suits the conditions.
- Make sure the full lighting system of your vehicle is turned on.
- Use your low-beam headlights. High beams reflect off the moisture droplets in the fog, making it harder to see.
- If you have fog lights on your vehicle, use them, in addition to your low beams.
- Be patient. Avoid passing, changing lanes and crossing traffic.
- Use pavement markings to help guide you. Use the right edge of the road as a guide, rather than the centre line.

- Increase your following distance. You will need extra distance to brake safely.
- Look and listen for any hazards that may be ahead.
- Reduce the distractions in your vehicle. For example, turn off the cell phone. Your full attention is required.
- Watch for any electronically operated warning signs.
- Keep looking as far ahead as possible.
- Keep your windows and mirrors clean. Use your defroster and wipers to maximize your vision.
- If the fog is too dense to continue, pull completely off the road and try to position your vehicle in a safe parking area. Turn on your emergency flashers, in addition to keeping your low-beam headlights on.

DON'T

- Don't stop on the travelled portion of the road. You could become

the first link in a chain-reaction collision.
- Don't speed up suddenly, even if the fog seems to be clearing. You could find yourself suddenly back in fog.
- Don't speed up to pass a vehicle moving slowly or to get away from a vehicle that is following too closely.

REMEMBER

- Watch your speed. You may be going faster than you think. If so, reduce speed gradually.
- Leave a safe braking distance between you and the vehicle ahead.
- Remain calm and patient. Don't pass other vehicles or speed up suddenly.
- Don't stop on the road. If visibility is decreasing rapidly, pull off the road into a safe parking area and wait for the fog to lift.
- When visibility is reduced, use your low-beam lights.

Rain

Rain makes road surfaces slippery, especially as the first drops fall. With more rain, tires make less contact with the road. If there is too much water or if you are going too fast, your tires may ride on top of the water, like water skis. This is called hydroplaning. When this happens, control becomes very difficult. Make sure you have good tires with deep tread, and slow down when the road is wet.

Rain also reduces visibility. Drive slowly enough to be able to stop within the distance you can see. Make sure your windshield wipers are in good condition. If your wiper blades do not clean the windshield without streaking, replace them.

In rain, try to drive on clear sections of road. Look ahead and plan your movements. Smooth steering, braking and accelerating will reduce the chance of skids. Leave more space between you and

the vehicle ahead in case you have to stop. This will also help you to avoid spray from the vehicle ahead that can make it even harder to see.

Avoid driving in puddles. A puddle can hide a large pothole that could damage your vehicle or its suspension, or flatten a tire. The spray of water could obstruct the vision of adjacent motorists and result in a collision, cause harm to nearby pedestrians or drown your engine, causing it to stall. Water can also make your brakes less effective.

Flooded roads

Avoid driving on flooded roads—water may prevent your brakes from working. If you must drive through a flooded stretch of road, test your brakes afterward to dry them out.

Test your brakes when it is safe to do so by stopping quickly and firmly at 50 km/h. Make sure the vehicle stops in a straight line, without pulling to one side. The brake

pedal should feel firm and secure, not spongy–that's a sign of trouble. If you still feel a pulling to one side or a spongy brake pedal even after the brakes are dry, you should take the vehicle in for repair immediately.

Skids

A skid may happen when one or more tires lose their grip with the road's surface. Skids most often happen on a slippery surface, such as a road that is wet, icy or covered with snow, gravel or some other loose material. Most skids result from driving too fast for road conditions. Hard braking and overly aggressive turning or accelerating can cause your vehicle to skid and possibly go out of control.

To avoid a skid on a slippery road, drive at a reduced speed and operate the vehicle's controls in a smooth and constrained manner. Increasing tire forces, such as by braking or accelerating while steering may push tires even closer to a skid condition. It's essential that the vehicle's speed be maintained at a safe level and that turns be made gently.

If your vehicle begins to skid, try not to panic—it is possible to maintain control of your vehicle, even in a skid. Ease off on the accelerator or brake and on a very slippery surface slip the transmission into neutral if you can. Continue to steer in the direction you wish to go. Be careful not to oversteer. Once you regain control, you can brake as needed, but very gently and smoothly.

Anti-lock braking systems (ABS)

If your vehicle is equipped with anti-lock brakes, practise emergency braking to understand how your vehicle will react. It is a good idea to practise doing this under controlled conditions with a qualified driving instructor.

ABS is designed to sense the speed of the wheels on a vehicle during braking. An abnormal drop in wheel speed, which indicates potential wheel lock, causes the brake force to be reduced to that wheel. This is how ABS prevents tire skid and the accompanying loss of steering control. This improves vehicle safety during heavy brake use or when braking with poor traction.

Although anti-lock braking systems help to prevent wheel lock, you should not expect the stopping distance for your vehicle to be shortened.

Drivers unfamiliar with anti-lock braking may be surprised by the pulsations that they may feel in the brake pedal when they brake hard. Make sure you know what to expect so you will not be distracted by the pulsation or tempted to release the pedal during emergency braking manoeuvres.

Threshold braking–Threshold braking should bring you to a reasonably quick controlled stop in your own lane, even in slippery conditions. This technique is generally practised in a vehicle that is not equipped with ABS. Brake as hard as you can until a wheel begins to lock up, then release pressure on the pedal slightly to release the wheel. Press down on the brake pedal, applying as much braking force as possible without inducing a skid. If you feel any of the wheels begin to lock up, release the brake pressure slightly and re-apply. Don't pump the brakes. Continue braking this way until you have slowed the vehicle to the desired speed.

Vehicles equipped with ABS should provide controlled braking on slippery surfaces automatically. Press the brake pedal hard and allow the system to control wheel lock-up. (See page 36 for details on engine retarders.)

TIPS FOR DRIVING IN BLOWING SNOW AND WHITEOUT CONDITIONS

Before you drive—and during your trip—check weather forecasts and road reports. If there is a weather warning, or reports of poor visibility and driving conditions, delay your trip until conditions improve, if possible. If you get caught driving in blowing snow or a whiteout, follow these safe driving tips:

DO:
- Slow down gradually and drive at a speed that suits the conditions.
- Make sure the full lighting system of your vehicle is turned on.
- Use your low-beam headlights. High beams reflect off the ice particles in the snow, making it harder to see.
- If you have fog lights on your vehicle, use them, in addition to your low beams.
- Be patient. Avoid passing, changing lanes and crossing traffic.
- Increase your following distance. You will need extra space to brake safely.

- Stay alert. Keep looking as far ahead as possible.
- Reduce the distractions in your vehicle. Your full attention is required.
- Keep your windows and mirrors clean. Use defroster and wipers to maximize your vision.
- Try to get off the road when visibility is near zero. Pull into a safe parking area if possible.

DON'T
- Don't stop on the travelled portion of the road. You could become the first link in a chain-reaction collision.
- Don't attempt to pass a vehicle moving slowly or speed up to get away from a vehicle that is following too closely.

REMEMBER
- Watch your speed. You may be going faster than you think. If so, reduce speed gradually.

- Leave a safe braking distance between you and the vehicle ahead.
- Stay alert, remain calm and be patient.
- If visibility is decreasing rapidly, do not stop on the road. Look for an opportunity to pull off the road into a safe parking area and wait for conditions to improve.
- If you become stuck or stranded in severe weather, stay with your vehicle for warmth and safety until help arrives. Open a window slightly for ventilation. Run your motor sparingly. Use your emergency flashers.
- Be prepared and carry a winter driving survival kit that includes items such as warm clothing, non-perishable energy foods, flashlight, shovel and blanket.
- It is important to look ahead and watch for clues that indicate you need to slow down and anticipate slippery road conditions.

Snow

Snow may be hard-packed and slippery as ice; rutted and full of tracks and gullies; or it can be smooth and soft. Look ahead and anticipate what you must do based on the conditions. Slow down on rutted snowy roads. Avoid sudden steering, braking or accelerating that could cause a skid.

Whiteouts

Blowing snow may create whiteouts where snow completely blocks your view of the road. When blowing snow is forecast, drive only if necessary and with extreme caution.

Ice

As temperatures drop below freezing, wet roads become icy. Sections of road in shaded areas or on bridges and overpasses freeze first. It is important to look ahead, slow down and anticipate ice.

If the road ahead looks like black and shiny asphalt, be suspicious. It may be covered by a thin layer of ice known as black ice. Generally, asphalt in the winter should look gray-white in colour. If you think there may be black ice ahead, slow down and be careful.

Snow plows

Flashing blue lights warn you of wide and slow-moving snow removal vehicles: some snow plows have a wing that extends as far as three metres to the right of the vehicle. On freeways, several snow plows may be staggered across the road, clearing all lanes at the same time by passing a ridge of snow from plow to plow. Do not try to pass between them. This is extremely dangerous because there is not enough room to pass safely, and the ridge of wet snow can throw your vehicle out of control.

Chapter 3, section I-Summary
By the end of this section, you should know:
- How to identify and manage situations where your visibility may be reduced
- How weather conditions such as rain, flooded roads, snow and ice may affect your vehicle and your ability to control it
- What to do if your vehicle skids or if you encounter heavy snow, whiteouts or black ice
- How to recognize and share the road with snow removal vehicles

II. DEALING WITH PARTICULAR SITUATIONS

Drowsy driving

Drowsiness has been identified as a causal factor in a growing number of collisions resulting in injury and fatality. Tired drivers can be as impaired as drunk drivers. They have a slower reaction time and are less alert.

Studies have shown that collisions involving drowsiness tend to occur during late night/early morning hours (between 2 a.m. and 6 a.m.) or late afternoon (between 2 p.m. and 4 p.m.). Studies also indicate that shift workers, people with undiagnosed or untreated sleep disorders, and commercial vehicle operators are at greater risk for such collisions.

Always avoid driving when you are feeling drowsy. Scientific research confirms that you can fall asleep without actually being aware of it. Here are eight important warning signs that your drowsiness is serious enough to place you at risk:

- You have difficulty keeping your eyes open.
- Your head keeps tilting forward despite your efforts to keep your eyes on the road.
- Your mind keeps wandering and you can't seem to concentrate.
- You yawn frequently.
- You can't remember details about the last few kilometres you have travelled.
- You are missing traffic lights and signals.
- Your vehicle drifts into the next lane and you have to jerk it back into your lane.
- You have drifted off the road and narrowly avoided a crash.

If you have one of these symptoms, you may be in danger of falling asleep. Pull off the road and park your vehicle in a safe, secure place. Use well-lit rest stops or truck stops on busy roads. Stimulants are never a substitute for sleep. Drinks containing caffeine can help you feel more alert, but if you are sleep deprived, the effects wear off quickly. The same is true of turning up the volume of your radio or CD player and opening the window. You cannot trick your body into staying awake; you need to sleep. Remember, the only safe driver is a well-rested, alert driver.

Workers on the road

Be extra careful when driving through construction zones and areas where people are working on or near the road.

When approaching a construction zone, proceed with caution and obey all warning signs, people and/or devices that are directing traffic through the area. Often, lower-speed limits are posted to increase worker safety and reflect increased road hazards, such as construction vehicles in the area, uneven or gravel surfaces, narrowed lanes and so on. In a construction zone, drive carefully and adjust your driving to suit the conditions. Do not change lanes, be ready for sudden stops and watch for workers and related construction vehicles and equipment on the road.

Other types of workers and vehicles may also be present on the road and pose a hazard, such as road-side assistance and disabled vehicles, surveyors, road maintenance or utility workers. Always slow down and pass with caution to prevent a collision. If safe to do so, move over a lane to increase the space between your vehicle and the hazard.

Traffic-control workers direct vehicle traffic in work zones and prevent conflicts between construction activity and traffic. Whether you are driving during the day or at night, watch for traffic-control people and follow their instructions.

Treat people working on roads with respect, and be patient if traffic is delayed. Sometimes traffic in one direction must wait while

vehicles from the other direction pass through a detour. If your lane is blocked and no one is directing traffic, yield to the driver coming from the opposite direction. When the way is clear, move slowly and carefully around the obstacle.

Recent changes to the *Highway Traffic Act* have resulted in doubled fines for speeding in a construction zone when workers are present. It is also an offence to disobey **STOP** or **SLOW** signs displayed by a traffic-control person or firefighter.

Animals on the road

You may come upon farm animals or wild animals on the road, especially in farming areas and in the northern parts of the province. Animal-crossing signs warn drivers where there is a known danger of moose, deer or cattle stepping onto the road, but animals may appear anywhere. Always be alert for animals and ready to react.

Look well ahead. At night, use your high beams where possible. When you see an animal, brake or slow down if you can without risk to vehicles behind you. If there is no traffic and no danger of colliding with any other object, steer around the animal, staying in control of your vehicle.

In some areas of the province, horse-drawn carriages may use the road. Be prepared to share the road with them.

Distracted driving

Commercial passenger-vehicle and school-bus drivers need to be aware of potential situations that may distract them from driving. Some distractions occur outside the bus, such as police activity, collisions, scenery or road construction.

Drivers can also be distracted by situations inside the vehicle. In particular, school-bus drivers deal with high levels of noise and activity. If a driver has to take his or her eyes off the road in order to address a behavioural issue, there is a greater risk of collision.

Even if your vehicle has driver-assistance features, you can be charged with distracted, careless or dangerous driving. You are still expected to be in care and control of your vehicle, which means you must be constantly monitoring your environment and able to take over immediate control of the vehicle.

Driving while using non-hands-free cellular phones and viewing display screens unrelated to driving is prohibited, and drivers will face fines and other penalties. In addition, drivers can be charged with careless driving or even dangerous driving (a criminal offence) if they do not pay full attention to the driving task.

Commercial drivers have a permanent exemption for the use of a two-way radio, provided the microphone is securely mounted to the vehicle within easy reach of the driver. This allows the driver to press and hold the microphone button to talk and release to listen.

Note: Bus and transit drivers have been provided with a temporary exemption allowing them to use hand-held, two-way radios until January 1, 2021.

TIPS TO REDUCE DRIVER DISTRACTIONS

- Attend to personal grooming and plan your route before you leave.
- Identify and preset your vehicle's climate control and audio settings.
- Make it a habit to pull over and park to use your cell phone, or have a passenger take the call or let it go to voice mail.
- Put reading material away if you are tempted to read.
- Do not engage in emotional or complex conversations. Stress can affect your driving performance.
- When you are hungry or thirsty, take a break from driving.

Remember to focus on your driving at all times. A split-second distraction behind the wheel can result in injury or even death.

Emergency Vehicles
Emergency vehicles include fire and police department vehicles, ambulances and public-utility emergency vehicles.

Reacting to an approaching emergency vehicle
When you see red or red **and** blue flashing lights, or hear the bells or sirens of an emergency vehicle approaching from either direction, you must immediately slow down, move as far to the right side of the roadway as you can, and stop.

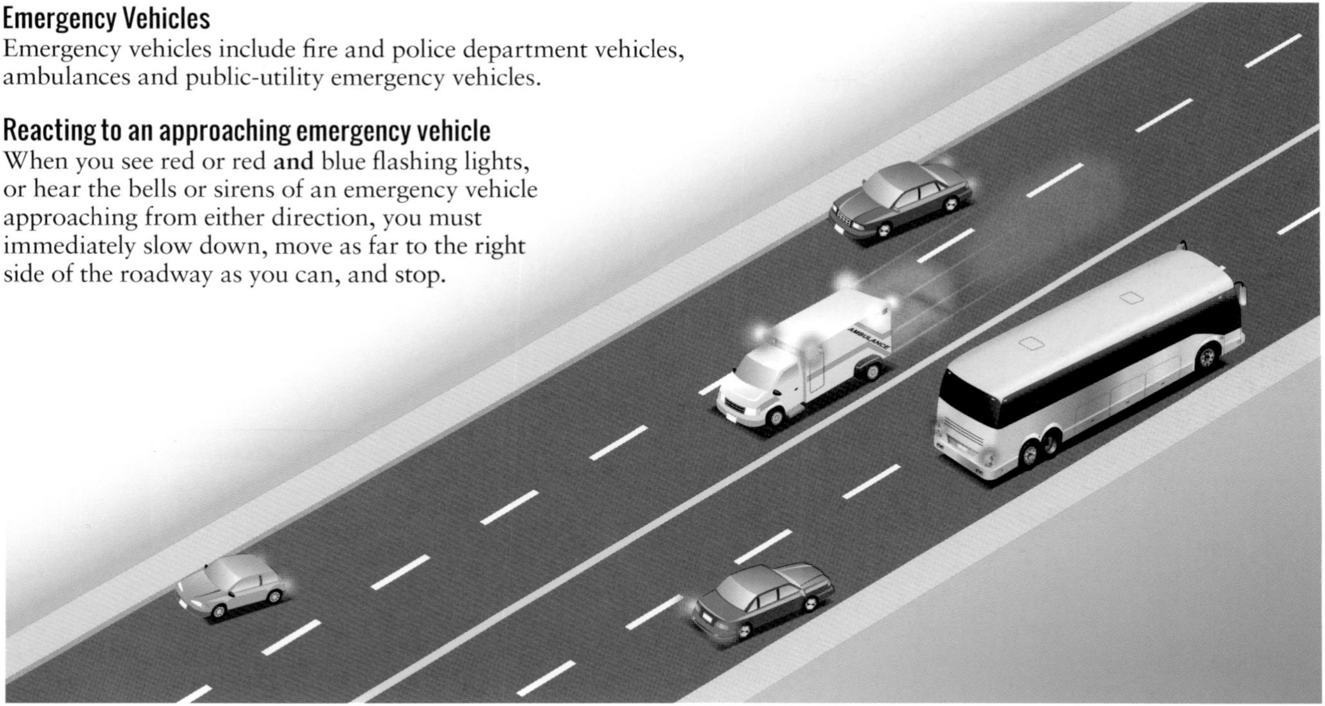

Diagram 3-1

Stay alert. When you see an approaching emergency vehicle with its lights or siren on, prepare to clear the way.

- React quickly but calmly. Don't slam on the brakes or pull over suddenly. Use your signals to alert other drivers you intend to pull over.
- Check your rearview mirrors. Look in front and on both sides of your vehicle. Allow other vehicles to also pull over. Pull to the right and gradually come to a stop.

- Wait for the emergency vehicle to pass and watch for other emergency vehicles that may be responding to the same call. Check to make sure the way is clear and signal before merging back into traffic.
- Don't drive on or block the shoulder on freeways. Emergency vehicles will use the shoulder of the road if all lanes are blocked.

Never follow or try to outrun an emergency vehicle. It is illegal to follow within 150 metres of a fire vehicle or ambulance responding to a call in any lane going in the same direction.

Failing to pull over and stop for an approaching emergency vehicle can result in a conviction and a fine.

Note: Some firefighters and volunteer medical responders may display a flashing green light when using their own vehicles to respond to a fire or medical emergency. Please yield the right-of-way to help them reach the emergency quickly and safely.

Take lights and sirens seriously. Clear the way! Pull to the right and stop. It's the law.

Reacting to a stopped emergency vehicle or tow truck

When you see an emergency vehicle stopped with its red, or red and blue, flashing lights or a stopped tow truck with its amber lights flashing in a lane or on the shoulder in your direction of travel, you must slow down and pass with caution. If the road has two or more lanes, you must move over into another lane to allow one lane clearance between your vehicle and the emergency vehicle, if it can be done safely.

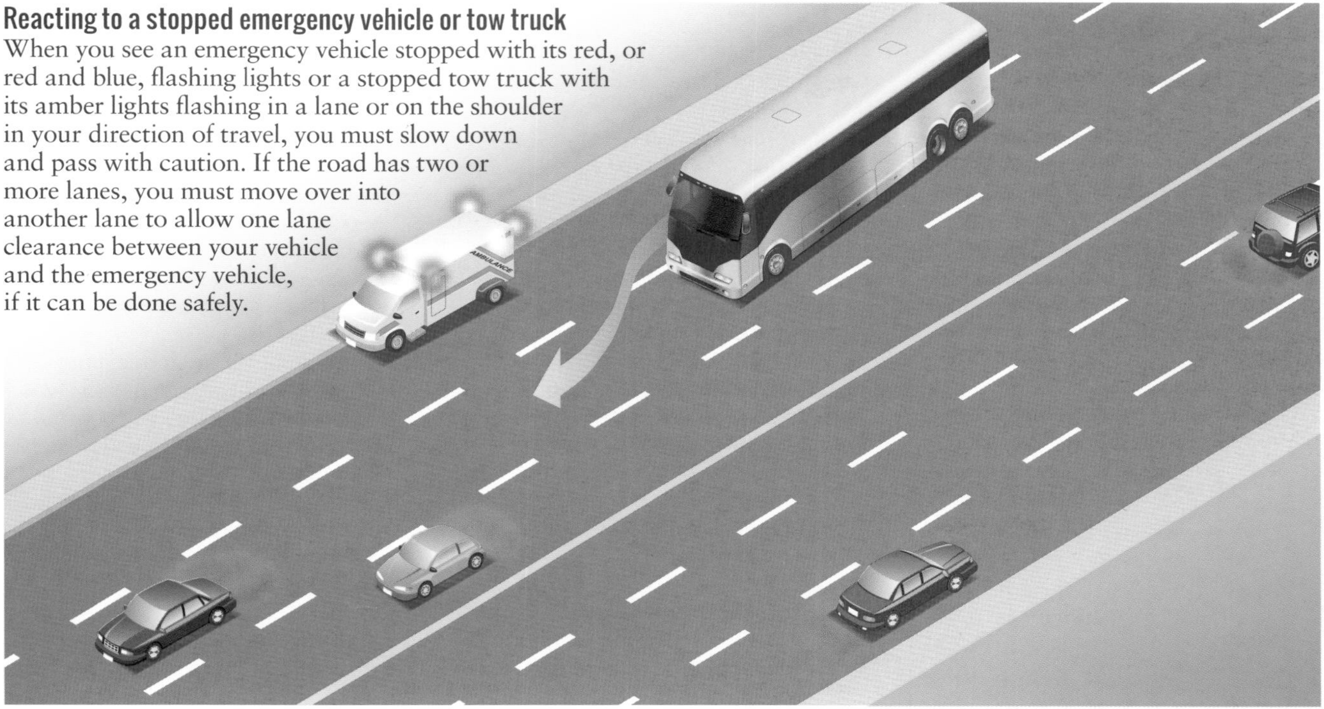

Diagram 3-2

Failing to follow these rules can result in a conviction, demerit points on your driving record, a driver'slicence suspension of up to two years and a fine of $400 to $2,000 for a first offence, and $1,000 to $4,000 for a subsequent offence (a "subsequent" offence is when you are convicted again within five years). The court can order you to spend up to six months in jail, or you may have to pay a fine or do both.

Chapter 3, section II-Summary
By the end of this section, you should know:
- How to recognize the signs and dangers of drowsy driving
- How to manoeuvre your vehicle through construction zones
- What to do if you encounter animals on the road
- Things that may distract you when driving and how to minimize those distractions
- What to do when you encounter an emergency vehicle

III. DEALING WITH EMERGENCIES
Stall or breakdown procedure
If the vehicle stalls or breaks down on the highway, quickly and calmly act to protect the passengers and other motorists.
- Stop as far off the roadway as possible.
- If you cannot find and repair the trouble, remain with the vehicle and ask a responsible person to find help.
- Set out appropriate flares, lamps, lanterns or portable reflectors as required by the *Highway Traffic Act* at a distance of approximately 30 metres (100 ft.) in advance of the vehicle and 30 metres (100 ft.) to the rear. They must be visible from 150 metres (500 ft.) in each direction.

In a collision where someone is injured

St. John Ambulance recommends that all drivers carry a well-stocked first-aid kit and know how to use it. School buses must be equipped with a first-aid kit. Consider reading a book about first aid or taking a course. It could mean the difference between life and death in a collision.

Every driver involved in a collision must stay at the scene or return to it immediately and give all possible assistance. If you are not personally involved in a collision, you should stop to offer help if police or other officials have not arrived.

In a collision with injuries, possible fuel leaks or serious vehicle damage, stay calm and follow these steps:

1. Call for help or have someone else call. By law, you must report any collision to the police when there are injuries or damage to vehicles or other property exceeding $2,000.

2. Turn off all engines and turn on emergency flashers. Set up warning signals or flares, and have someone warn approaching drivers.

3. Do not let anyone smoke, light a match or put flares near any vehicle, in case of a fuel leak. If any of the vehicles is on fire, get the people out and make sure everyone is well out of the way. If there is no danger of fire or explosion, leave injured people where they are until trained medical help arrives.

4. If you are trained in first aid, treat injuries in the order of urgency, within the level of your training. For example, clear the person's airway to restore breathing, give rescue breathing or stop bleeding by applying pressure with a clean cloth.

5. If you are not trained in first aid, use common sense. For example, people in collisions often go into shock. Cover the person with a jacket or blanket to reduce the effects of shock.

6. Stay with injured people until help arrives.

7. Disabled vehicles on the road may be a danger to you and other drivers. Do what you can to make sure everyone involved in a collision is kept safe.

In a collision where no one is injured

Follow these steps in a collision where there are no injuries:

1. If the vehicles are driveable, move them as far off the road as possible—this should not affect the police officer's investigation. This is especially important on busy or high-speed roads where it may be dangerous to leave vehicles in the driving lanes. If you cannot move the vehicles off the road, set up

warning signals or flares far enough away to give other traffic time to slow down or stop.

2. Call police (provincial or local, depending on where the collision takes place). By law, you must report any collision to the police where there are injuries or damage to vehicles or property exceeding $2,000.

3. Give all possible help to police or anyone whose vehicle has been damaged. This includes giving police your name and address, the name and address of the registered owner of the vehicle, the vehicle plate and permit number and the liability insurance card.

4. Get the names, addresses and phone numbers of all witnesses.

5. If damage is less than $2,000, you are still required by law to exchange information with anyone whose vehicle has been damaged. However, the collision does not have to be reported to the police.

6. Contact your insurance company as soon as possible if you intend to make a claim.

Fires

There are five common causes of vehicle fires:

1. Leaking fuel
2. Electrical shorts
3. Overheated brakes
4. Under-inflated/flat tire
5. Wheel-bearing failure.

All buses and school buses are required to carry an adequate fire extinguisher. Every driver should know how to use the fire extinguisher.

Remember in case of fire:

1. Remove passengers from the vehicle quickly and in an orderly manner.
2. Direct passengers to a safe place.

Chapter 3, section III-Summary
By the end of this section, you should know:

- What to do in emergency situations when your vehicle stalls or breaks down
- The steps to take if you are involved in a collision with or without injuries

CHAPTER 4
TRAFFIC SIGNS AND LIGHTS

Traffic laws include the signs and lights, pedestrian signals and pavement markings that tell drivers and other road users what they must do in certain situations. This chapter shows you what many of those signs, lights and markings look like, and explains what they mean to drivers.

I. SIGNS

Traffic signs give you important information about the law, warn you about dangerous conditions and help you find your way. Signs use different symbols, colours and shapes for easy identification.

Here are some of the many signs you will see on Ontario roads:

A stop sign is eight-sided and has a red background with white letters. It means you must come to a complete stop. Stop at the stop line if it is marked on the pavement. If there is no stop line, stop at the crosswalk. If there is no crosswalk, stop at the edge of the sidewalk. If there is no sidewalk, stop at the edge of the intersection. Wait until the way is clear before entering the intersection.

A school zone sign is five-sided and has a fluorescent yellow/green background with black symbols. It warns that you are coming to a school zone. Slow down, drive with extra caution and watch for children.

A yield sign is a triangle with a white background and a red border. It means you must let traffic in the intersection or close to it go first. Stop if necessary and go only when the way is clear.

A railway crossing sign is X-shaped with a white background and red outline. It warns that railway tracks cross the road. Watch for this sign. Slow down and look both ways for trains. Be prepared to stop.

There are four other kinds of signs: regulatory, warning, temporary conditions and information and direction.

Regulatory signs

These signs give a direction that must be obeyed. They are usually rectangular or square with a white or black background and black, white or coloured letters. A sign with a green circle means you may or must do the activity shown inside the ring. A red circle with a line through it means the activity shown is not allowed.

Here are some common regulatory signs:

This road is an official bicycle route. Watch for cyclists and be prepared to share the road with them.

You may park in the area between the signs during the times posted. (Used in pairs or groups.)

Snowmobiles may use this road.

Do not enter this road.

Do not stop in the area between the signs. This means you may not stop your vehicle in this area, even for a moment. (Used in pairs or groups.)

Do not stand in the area between the signs. This means you may not stop your vehicle in this area except while loading or unloading passengers. (Used in pairs or groups.)

Do not park in the area between the signs. This means you may not stop your vehicle except to load or unload passengers or merchandise. (Used in pairs or groups.)

Do not turn left at the intersection.

Do not drive through the intersection.

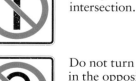

Do not turn to go in the opposite direction. (U-turn)

Do not turn right when facing a red light at the intersection.

Do not turn left during the times shown.

This parking space is only for vehicles displaying a valid Accessible Parking Permit.

No bicycles allowed on this road.

No pedestrians allowed on this road.

Keep to the right of the traffic island.

Speed limit changes ahead.

Do not pass on this road.

SLOWER TRAFFIC KEEP RIGHT

Slow traffic on multi-lane roads must keep right.

COMMUNITY SAFETY ZONE FINES INCREASED

Indicates areas where the community has identified that there is a special risk to pedestrians. Traffic related offences committed within the zone are subject to increased fines.

The speed limit in this zone is lower during school hours. Observe the speed limit shown when the yellow lights are flashing.

These signs, above the road or on the pavement before an intersection, tell drivers the direction they must travel. For example: the driver in lane one must turn left; the driver in lane two must turn left or go straight ahead; and the driver in lane three must turn right.

Traffic may travel in one direction only.

This is a pedestrian crossover. Be prepared to stop and yield right-of-way to pedestrians.

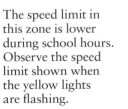

This sign, above the road or on the ground, means the lane is only for two-way left turns.

This sign reserves curb area for vehicles displaying a valid Accessible Parking Permit picking up and dropping off passengers with disabilities.

These signs mean lanes are only for specific types of vehicles, either all the time or during certain hours. Different symbols are used for the different types of vehicles. They include: buses, taxis, vehicles with three or more people and bicycles.

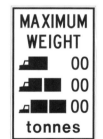

Keep to the right lane except when passing on two-lane sections where climbing or passing lanes are provided.

Indicates different weight restrictions for different types of heavy trucks for a bridge structure.

This sign on the back of transit buses serves as a reminder to motorists of the law requiring vehicles approaching a bus stopped at a dedicated Bus Stop to yield to the bus, once the bus has signalled its intent to return to the lane.

High Occupancy Vehicle (HOV) signs

Only public vehicles such as buses, or passenger vehicles carrying a specified minimum number of passengers, may use this lane.

Vehicles cannot change lanes into or out of a high-occupancy vehicle lane in this area.

Road forks to the right.

Marks a zone within which school buses load or unload passengers without using the red alternating lights and stop arm.

Warning signs

These signs warn of dangerous or unusual conditions ahead such as a curve, turn, dip or sideroad. They are usually diamond-shaped and have a yellow background with black letters or symbols.

Here are some common warning signs:

Maximum vertical clearance of 3.9 metres under this obstruction.

Slow down around this curve due to its smaller radius.

Indicates an upcoming bus entrance on the right and vehicles should be aware of buses entering the roadway.

 Indicates an upcoming fire truck entrance on the right, and drivers should be aware of fire trucks entering the roadway.

 Narrow bridge ahead.

 Road branching off ahead.

 Intersection ahead. The arrow shows which direction of traffic has the right-of-way.

Roundabout ahead. Reduce speed. The counter-clockwise arrows show the direction of vehicle traffic within the roundabout.

Drivers on the sideroad at the intersection ahead don't have a clear view of traffic.

 Slight bend or curve in the road ahead.

 Chevron (arrowhead) signs are posted in groups to guide drivers around sharp curves in the road.

 Pavement narrows ahead.

 Posted under a curve warning, this sign shows the maximum safe speed for the curve.

 Winding road ahead.

 Sharp bend or turn in the road ahead.

 The bridge ahead lifts or swings to let boats pass.

Paved surface
ends ahead.

Bicycle crossing
ahead.

Stop sign ahead.
Slow down.

Share the road with
oncoming traffic.

The share the road
sign is used to warn
motorists that they
are to provide safe
space on the road for
cyclists and other
vehicles.

Pavement is slippery
when wet. Slow
down and drive
with caution.

Hazard close to the
edge of the road.
The downward lines
show the side on
which you may
safely pass.

Divided highway
begins: traffic travels
in both directions
on separated roads
ahead. Keep to the
right-hand road.
Each road carries
one way traffic.

Right lane ends
ahead. If you are
in the right-hand
lane, you must merge
safely with traffic in
the lane to the left.

Traffic lights ahead. Slow down.

Steep hill ahead. You may need to use a lower gear.

Two roads going in the same direction are about to join into one. Drivers on both roads are equally responsible for seeing that traffic merges smoothly and safely.

Snowmobiles cross this road.

Divided highway ends: traffic travels in both directions on the same road ahead. Keep to the right-hand road.

Underpass ahead. Take care if you are driving a tall vehicle. Sign shows how much room you have.

Bump or uneven pavement on the road ahead. Slow down and keep control of your vehicle.

Railway crossing ahead. Be alert for trains. This sign also shows the angle at which the railway tracks cross the road.

Sharp turn or bend in the road in the direction of the arrow. The checkerboard border warns of danger. Slow down; be careful.

Deer regularly cross this road; be alert for animals.

Truck entrance on the right side of the road ahead. If the sign shows the truck on the left, the entrance is on the left side of the road.

Shows maximum safe speed on ramp.

Watch for pedestrians and be prepared to share the road with them.

Watch for fallen rock and be prepared to avoid a collision.

There may be water flowing over the road.

This sign warns you that you are coming to a hidden school bus stop. Slow down, drive with extra caution, watch for children and for a school bus with flashing red lights.

These signs warn of a school crossing. Watch for children and follow the directions of the crossing guard or school safety patroller.

Temporary condition signs

These signs warn of unusual temporary conditions such as road work zones, diversions, detours, lane closures or traffic-control people on the road. They are usually diamond-shaped with an orange background and black letters or symbols.

Here are some common temporary condition signs:

 Construction work one kilometre ahead.

 Road work ahead.

 Survey crew working on the road ahead.

 Traffic control person ahead. Drive slowly and watch for instructions.

You are entering a construction zone. Drive with extra caution and be prepared for a lower speed limit.

 Temporary detour from normal traffic route.

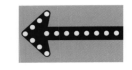 Flashing lights on the arrows show the direction to follow.

Pavement has been milled or grooved. Your vehicle's stopping ability may be affected so obey the speed limit and drive with extra caution. Motorcyclists may experience reduced traction on these surfaces.

 Lane ahead is closed for roadwork. Obey the speed limit and merge with traffic in the open lane.

Closed lane. Adjust speed to merge with traffic in lane indicated by arrow.

SPEED FINES
DOUBLED
IN CONSTRUCTION
ZONES WHEN
WORKERS PRESENT

Enforces doubling the *HTA* fines for speeding in a designated construction zone when there are workers present.

KITCHENER 72
LONDON   164

Shows the distances in kilometres to towns and cities on the road.

Do not pass the pilot or pace vehicle bearing this sign.

Information and direction signs

These signs tell you about distances and destinations. They are usually rectangular with a green background and white letters. Other signs with different colours guide you to facilities, services and attractions.

Here are some common information and direction signs:

Reduce speed and be prepared to stop.

Brennon Street

Various exit signs are used on freeways. In urban areas, many exit ramps have more than one lane. Overhead and ground-mounted signs help drivers choose the correct lane to exit or stay on the freeway.

Emily Street   EXIT

Advance signs use arrows to show which lanes lead off the freeway. Signs are also posted at the exit.

FOLLOW   DETOUR D-1

Follow detour marker until you return to regular route.

↑ BARRIE
← ORILLIA
MIDLAND ➡

Shows directions to nearby towns and cities.

Sometimes one or more lanes may lead off the freeway. The arrows matching the exit lanes are shown on the advance sign in a yellow box with the word 'exit' under them.

Freeway interchanges or exits have numbers that correspond to the distance from the beginning of the freeway. For example, interchange number 204 on Highway 401 is 204 kilometres from Windsor, where the freeway begins. Distances can be calculated by subtracting one interchange number from another.

The term "VIA" is used to describe the roads that must be followed to reach a destination.

Shows the upcoming roundabout exists and where they will take you.

EXPRESS MOVING SLOWLY COLLECTOR MOVING WELL BEYOND NEXT TRANSFER

These signs change according to traffic conditions to give drivers current information on delays and lane closures ahead.

Shows off-road facilities such as hospitals, airports, universities or carpool lots.

Shows route to passenger railway station.

Shows route to airport.

Shows facilities that are accessible by wheelchair.

D sign - Oversize load

Other signs

Here are some other common signs:

The "slow-moving vehicle" sign is an orange triangle with a red border. It alerts other drivers that the vehicle ahead will be travelling at 40 km/h or less. When on a road, farm tractors, farm implements/machinery, and vehicles not capable of sustaining speeds over 40 km/h must display the slow moving vehicle sign. Watch for these slow moving vehicles and reduce your speed as necessary.

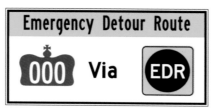

EDR signs are used during the unscheduled closure of a provincial highway when OPP detour all traffic off the highway. The EDR markers are located along alternative routes and provide direction to motorists around the closure and back onto the highway.

Long commercial vehicle (LCV)

This placard indicates a long commercial vehicle, which is a double trailer and can be up to 40 metres in length. It is important to be able to recognize an LCV on the highway, based on rear signage, and anticipate both extended length and limited speed when preparing to pass one on the highway.

Emergency response signs

Some information-tion signs include a numbering system along the bottom of the sign to assist emergency vehicles and drivers in determining an appropriate route.

Bilingual signs

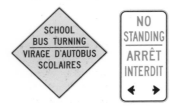

Watch for these signs when driving in designated bilingual areas. Read the messages in the language you understand best. Bilingual messages may be together on the same sign or separate, with an English sign immediately followed by a French sign.

II. TRAFFIC LIGHTS

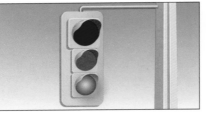

Traffic lights tell drivers and pedestrians what they must do at intersections and along roads. They tell road users when to stop and go, when and how to turn and when to drive with extra caution.

Green light

A green light means you may turn left, go straight or turn right after yielding to vehicles and pedestrians already in the intersection. When turning left or right you must yield the right-of-way to pedestrians crossing the intersection.

Yellow light

A yellow—or amber—light means the red light is about to appear. You must stop if you can do so safely; otherwise, go with caution.

Red light

A red light means you must stop. Bring your vehicle to a complete stop at the stop line if it is marked on the pavement. If there is no stop line, stop at the crosswalk, marked or not. If there is no crosswalk, stop at the edge of the sidewalk. If there is no sidewalk, stop at the edge of the intersection.

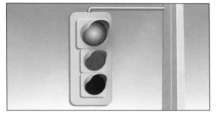

Wait until the light changes to green and the intersection is clear before moving through it.

Unless a sign tells you not to, you may turn right on a red light only after coming to a complete stop and waiting until the way is clear. You may also turn left on a red light if you are moving from a one-way road onto a one-way road, but you must come to a complete stop first and wait until the way is clear.

Lights and arrows to help turning vehicles

Flashing green lights and green arrows direct drivers who are turning.

Advance green light or arrow

When you face a flashing green light or a left-pointing green arrow and a green light, you may turn left, go straight ahead or turn right from the proper lane. This is called an advanced green light because oncoming traffic still faces a red light.

Pedestrians must not cross on a flashing green light unless a pedestrian signal tells them to.

Simultaneous left turn

When a left-turn green arrow is shown with a red light, you may turn left from the left-turn lane. Vehicles turning left from the opposite direction may also be making left turns because they too face a left-turn green arrow.

After the left-turn green arrow, a yellow arrow may appear. This means the green light is about to appear for traffic in one or both directions. Do not start your left turn. Stop if you can do so safely; otherwise, complete your turn with caution.

You can still turn left when the light is green, but only when the way is clear of traffic and pedestrians. If the light turns red when you are in the intersection, complete your turn when it is safe.

Pedestrians must not cross on a left-turn green arrow unless a pedestrian signal tells them to.

Transit Priority Signals

Traffic and pedestrians must yield to public transit vehicles at a transit priority signal. The round signal is on top of a regular traffic signal and shows a white vertical bar on a dark background. This allows transit vehicles to go through, turn right or left, while all conflicting traffic faces a red light.

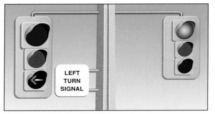

Fully protected left turn

Some intersections have separate traffic lights for left-turning traffic and for traffic going through the intersection or turning right.

When a left-turn green arrow appears for traffic in the left-turn lane, traffic going straight ahead or turning right will usually see a red light. You may turn left from the left-turn lane when you face a green arrow. Vehicles from the opposite direction may also be turning left.

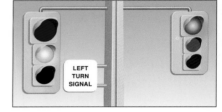

After the left-turn green arrow, a yellow light appears for left-turning vehicles only.

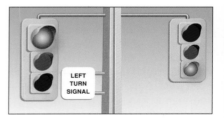

After the yellow light, a red light appears for left-turning vehicles only. Traffic going straight ahead or turning right will face a green light or green arrows pointing straight ahead and to the right.

In these intersections, you may not begin turning left after the green light appears for traffic going straight ahead or turning right. If the light turns yellow while you are in the intersection, complete your turn with caution.

Flashing red light
You must come to a complete stop at a flashing red light. Move through the intersection only when it is safe.

Flashing yellow light
A flashing yellow light means you should drive with caution when approaching and moving through the intersection.

Blank traffic lights
During an electrical power loss, traffic lights at intersections will not work. Yield the right-of-way to vehicles in the intersection and to vehicles entering the intersection from your right. Go cautiously and use the intersection the same way you would use an intersection with all-way stop signs.

Traffic beacons
A traffic beacon is a single flashing light hung over an intersection or placed over signs or on obstacles in the road.

Flashing red beacon
A flashing red beacon above an intersection or stop sign means you must come to a complete stop. Move through the intersection only when it is safe to do so.

Flashing yellow beacon
A flashing yellow beacon above an intersection, above a warning sign or on an obstruction in the road, warns you to drive with caution.

III. PEDESTRIAN SIGNALS

Pedestrian signals help pedestrians cross at intersections with traffic lights. The signal for pedestrians to walk is a white walking symbol. A flashing or steady orange hand symbol means pedestrians must not begin to cross.

A pedestrian facing a walk signal may cross the road in the direction of the signal. While crossing, pedestrians have the right-of-way over all vehicles.

A pedestrian facing a flashing or steady hand symbol should not begin to cross the road. Pedestrians who have already begun to cross when the hand signal appears should go as quickly as possible to a safe area. While they are crossing, pedestrians still have the right-of-way over vehicles.

At intersections with traffic lights where there are no pedestrian signals, pedestrians facing a green light may cross. Pedestrians may not cross on a flashing green light or a left-turn green arrow.

Intersection pedestrian signals

On a busy main road, an intersection pedestrian signal helps people to cross the road safely by signalling traffic to stop. The intersection pedestrian signal has one or more crosswalks, pedestrian walk and don't walk signals, push buttons for pedestrians, and traffic signal lights on the main road only.

Stop signs control traffic on the smaller, less busy crossroad.

You must observe, obey the traffic rules, and use your safe driving skills to drive through these intersections. (See Yielding the right-of-way on page 42.)

IV. PAVEMENT MARKINGS

Pavement markings work with road signs and traffic lights to give you important information about the direction of traffic and where you may and may not travel. Pavement markings divide traffic lanes, show turning lanes, mark pedestrian crossings, indicate obstacles, and tell you when it is not safe to pass.

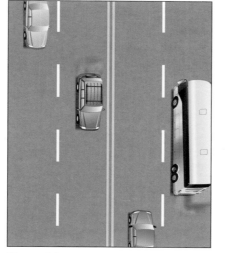

Diagram 4-1
Yellow lines separate traffic travelling in opposite directions. White lines separate traffic travelling in the same direction.

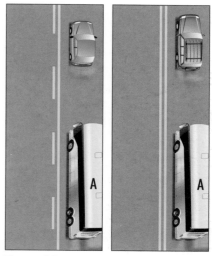

Diagram 4-2
A solid line at the left of your lane means it is unsafe to pass. ("A" should not pass.)

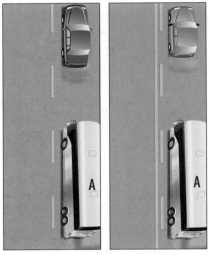

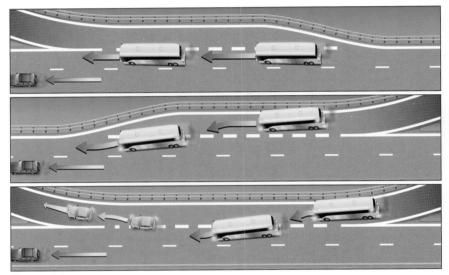

Diagram 4-3

A broken line at the left of your lane means you may pass if the way is clear. ("A" may pass if there are enough broken lines ahead to complete the pass safely.)

Diagram 4-4

Broken lines that are wider and closer together than regular broken lines are called continuity lines. When you see continuity lines on your left side, it generally means the lane you are in is ending or exiting, and that you must change lanes if you want to continue in your current direction. Continuity lines that appear only on your right mean your lane will continue unaffected.

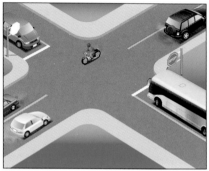

Diagram 4-5
A stop line is a single white line painted across the road at an intersection. It shows where you must stop. If there is no stop line marked on the road, stop at the crosswalk, marked or not. If there is no crosswalk, stop at the edge of the sidewalk. If there is no sidewalk, stop at the edge of the intersection.

Diagram 4-6
A crosswalk is marked by two parallel white lines painted across the road. However, crosswalks at intersections are not always marked. If there is no stop line, stop at the crosswalk, marked or not. If there is no crosswalk, stop at the edge of the sidewalk. If there is no sidewalk, stop at the edge of the intersection.

Diagram 4-7
A white arrow painted on a lane means you may move only in the direction of the arrow.

Diagram 4-8
A pedestrian crossing–or crossover
–is marked by two white double
parallel lines across the road with
an X in each lane approaching it.
Stop before the line and yield
to pedestrians.

Diagram 4-9
Two solid lines painted on the
pavement guide traffic away from
fixed objects such as bridge piers
or concrete islands. Usually a sign
is affixed to the object, and the
object is painted with yellow and
black markings.

Chapter 4-Summary

By the end of this chapter, you should know:

Signs
- The difference between regulatory, warning, temporary condition and information/direction signs
- How to read the symbols and messages of some common signs in each category

Traffic Lights
- The different colours and symbols that appear on traffic lights and what those mean
- How to navigate turns using advanced green lights and arrows
- How to proceed when approaching flashing amber or red lights
- What to do in situations where the traffic lights are not operating

Pedestrian Signals
- What the symbols on pedestrian signals indicate
- What an intersection pedestrian signal is and what to do if you encounter one

Pavement Markings
- How pavement markings are used to control traffic
- What the different colours and types of markings are used to indicate

CHAPTER 5
OPERATING A SCHOOL BUS

I. LOADING AND UNLOADING PASSENGERS

As a school-bus driver, it is your responsibility to ensure the safety of your passengers. This is especially important to remember when you are loading or unloading your passengers, as these are the times at which they are most vulnerable.

"Spotters," or safety patrollers, may help the school-bus driver when loading or unloading a school bus. The spotter can prevent the driver from hitting children who may have stopped in a blind area in front of the vehicle.

Recently developed safety equipment includes newly designed mirrors or multiple mirror-adjustment systems, motion-detector systems, bumper-mounted crossing barriers, and perimeter braking systems. When drivers and passengers are trained to use them effectively, they will enhance safety.

Keep the following rules in mind:
- Turn on the upper, alternating red signal lights before stopping to load or unload your passengers.
- As soon as the bus is stopped, extend the stop arm and the pedestrian student safety crossing arm.
- Remain stopped with the lights flashing and the stop and crossing arms extended until all passengers who must cross the highway have done so.
- Do not load or unload passengers on a steep grade or curve. You should have a clear view of the road in each direction for at least 150 metres (500 ft.).
- Stop on the travelled portion of the roadway and not the shoulder to load or unload passengers.

- Never load the bus beyond its licensed capacity.
- As a final step in loading passengers, you must ensure that all traffic has stopped before signalling students to board.

Loading or unloading passengers at traffic-signal lights

When loading or unloading at traffic-signal lights, do not activate the upper, alternating red flashing lights and stop arm on the school bus. The stop should be made as close as possible to the intersection, close to the curb or edge of the roadway, and the passengers cautioned to obey the traffic-signal lights.

If a driver needs to stop near an intersection with traffic-signal lights and use the flashing red lights and stop arm, the stop should be made at least 60 metres from the intersection.

School-bus loading zones

School bus loading zones are areas of a roadway or school driveway designated as passenger loading/unloading zones by signs that set out the limits of the zones.

In school-bus loading zones, stop the bus close to the right curb or edge of the roadway between the signs setting out the limits of the zone.

Keep in mind these two important rules of school-bus loading zones:

1. **Do not** operate the flashing lights and stop arm within a school-bus loading zone.
2. **Do not** stop your bus to load or unload passengers on the opposite side of the highway from a school-bus loading zone.

Rules for passengers

As the driver, you must ensure that your passengers observe the following rules:

- Upon entering the bus, passengers should go directly to their seats and sit down. All passengers should be seated before you move the bus again.
- Passengers should not enter or leave the bus while it is moving
- Passengers should not obstruct the vision of the driver to the front, sides or rear.
- Passengers should stay seated until the bus has come to a full stop.
- Passengers leaving the vehicle should cross only in front of the bus and approximately three metres (10 ft.) from the front of the bus, using the safety crossing arm as a guide.
- When more than one student leaves the bus, students should form a group in the front of the bus and on the right shoulder or curb of the road; the group should then look for the driver's signal indicating it is safe to cross.
- Passengers who remain on the right side of the stopped bus should form a group and stay together, away from the front right corner of the bus, until the bus moves away.

- Passengers should look both ways before stepping into the roadway, and continue to watch for traffic as they cross.
- Passengers should always cross the roadway at a right angle to the bus, never diagonally.
- Passengers should walk, never run, when crossing the roadway.

Note: Before driving off, you should check the convex cross-over mirrors to ensure that no passengers are crossing in front of the school bus.

II. SPECIAL SAFETY PRECAUTIONS FOR SCHOOL BUS DRIVERS

- When the bus is moving, the doors should be safely closed, but must not be locked.
- Do not allow passengers to obstruct your vision to the front, sides or rear.
- Never permit an unauthorized person to sit in the driver's seat, operate the vehicle or any of its controls.
- No lunch pails, books or parcels should be in the aisles or step wells at any time.
- Never leave the vehicle without first stopping the engine, setting the brakes, putting the transmission on its lowest gear or park position and removing the ignition key. Some automatic transmission vehicles do not have a "park" position. If this is the case, the vehicle should be parked with the transmission in "neutral" and the parking brake set.

- When a school bus is disabled on a roadway when lights are required, flares or reflectors must be placed 30 metres (100 ft.) in front and behind the vehicle.
- When loading and unloading students, and you cannot account for one, you should first secure the bus and check around and underneath the bus.

Reversing a school bus

Use care and caution when you are backing a school bus. Use the rear-view mirror, turn and look back and have someone give directions. The spotter must stand behind the bus and be visible to the driver in the mirror. If a spotter is not available, the driver must leave the bus and check the vehicle path for obstructions. Upon returning inside the bus, open the window and listen while backing slowly and cautiously. Being alert and watching traffic conditions around the vehicle at all times. Drivers should not back up their vehicles on school grounds or at loading or unloading stops, or zones without proper guidance and signals from a responsible person outside the bus.

Stopping at railway crossings

School buses must stop at least five metres (16.5 ft.) from the nearest rail at all railway crossings. While stopped, the driver must open the bus door and look and listen for any approaching trains. The driver must not change gears when the bus is actually crossing the tracks. The flashing lights and stop arm must not be activated in this situation.

When stopped for a period of time waiting at an intersection or railway crossing, it is a safe practice to place the gear-shift lever in neutral and release the clutch. Always set the parking brake.

III. STOPPING-FOR-SCHOOL-BUSES LAW
Stopping requirements

The stopping-for-school-buses law applies everywhere, regardless of the posted speed limit—on highways, county roads, city, town or village streets.

Motorists meeting (approaching from the opposite direction) a stopped school bus with its overhead red signal lights flashing, must stop before reaching the bus and shall not proceed until the bus moves or the overhead lights have stopped flashing. The only exception is on highways divided by a median; drivers on the other side of the median approaching from the opposite are not required to stop. (A median is a raised, lowered or earth strip dividing a road where vehicles travel in both directions.)

Diagram 5-1

Motorists approaching a stopped school bus from the rear with its overhead red signals lights flashing, shall stop at least 20 metres before reaching the bus and shall not proceed until the bus moves, or the overhead lights have stopped flashing.

Drivers who don't stop for a school bus can be fined $400 to $2,000 and get six demerit points for a first offence. If you break the rule a second time within five years, the penalty is a fine of $1,000 to $4,000 and six demerit points. You could also go to jail for up to six months.

If the driver is not charged, the vehicle's registered owner can be fined $400 to $2,000 for a first offence and $1,000 to $4,000 for subsequent offences within a five-year period if their vehicle illegally passes a school bus that is stopped with its red lights flashing. If the vehicle owner does not pay the fine, they will not be able to renew the vehicle's permit.

Stopping-for-school-buses law does not apply to all school-purposes buses

The school-bus stopping law only applies to chrome yellow school buses with proper markings and signals as defined in Section 175 of the *Highway Traffic Act* and only when loading or unloading adults with developmental disabilities or children. Drivers of other school-purposes vehicles must remember that they do not have the protection of this law, and be very careful when choosing places to stop and directing their passengers as they leave the bus.

20 Metres

Diagram 5-2

Reporting a school bus being passed

In Ontario, school bus drivers and other witnesses can report vehicles that have illegally passed a school bus. **The Illegal Passing of a School Bus Reporting Form** is available at the MTO website **www.mto.gov.on.ca**. This reporting form must be completed in its entirety before police action can be taken. You may also go to a police station to make a report. You may be required at a later date to attend court to provide evidence of what happened. A copy of the completed form may also be provided to a person charged with an offence so that he or she has a summary of what you will say in court. **The completed form should be delivered to your local police station as soon after the incident as possible.**

IV. EMERGENCY EVACUATION OF SCHOOL BUSES

It is important that you and your passengers know how to get out of the bus using the emergency exits, and how to use the safety equipment. It is also important that you inform authorities and request assistance if time allows.

It is your responsibility to set up a routine evacuation practice. In an emergency, practice can mean an orderly and speedy evacuation even if you are injured and unable to help. This practice should take place at the beginning of the school year and every month afterward.

Co-ordinate practice drills with the school administration and hold your drills in a safe, traffic-free area on school property.

The objective is to get the children off the bus safely in the shortest possible time and in an orderly way.

The standard emergency exits are:
- Front exit
- Rear exit
- Both front and rear
- Roof hatches and side push-out windows provide additional exits when needed; a driver must be aware of the use and operation

Evacuation procedure

1. Assess the situation. Generally, the quickest method is to use both front and rear doors. If those exits expose people to other dangers such as fire or traffic, choose the safest exit.
2. Remain calm. Speak loudly, but slowly. Ask the passengers to move calmly to the exit you choose.
3. Assign a responsible leader to count the passengers as they leave and lead them to a safe area away from the bus. The leader should keep everyone together.
4. Assign some taller students to wait at the rear exit on the ground at either side of the door to help as the students swing down. Another student inside tells the

exiting person to "watch your head, put your hands on the helper's shoulders and swing down."

5. While the other students remain in their seats, the students closest to danger should leave one seat at a time by walking to the exit.

6. All articles such as lunches, books and so on should be left behind.

7. As the last person leaves, walk the length of the bus to be sure everyone is out, and then exit yourself. Begin first-aid treatment if necessary. Assign two responsible students to go for help, if needed, and organize helpers to put out warning flares or reflectors as required.

Practice cannot eliminate all injury, but it will certainly reduce the possibility of unnecessary injury to yourself, your passengers and other motorists.

V. CARE AND MAINTENANCE OF A SCHOOL BUS
Mechanical fitness of school-purposes vehicles

Regulations under the *Highway Traffic Act* require regular inspection of every station wagon, van or bus operated by or under contract to a school board or other authority in charge of a school for the transportation of:

a) six or more adults with a developmental disability

b) six or more children

c) six or more persons referred to in a and b, between their homes and schools

Inspections are also required for a chrome yellow school bus transporting children between their homes and churches or adults with a developmental disability between their homes and training centres.

These vehicles must display valid inspection sticker(s).

The inspection must be carried out in a licensed motor-vehicle inspection station. Authorized inspection mechanics perform the inspection and affix stickers to vehicles found to be satisfactory.

School buses are subject to random safety inspections by Ministry of Transportation staff throughout the year.

A clean school bus

The driver should keep the vehicle clean. Passengers will take pride in a bus that is neat and clean, and will co-operate in keeping it that way.

Daily cleaning routine

The floor should be swept, and seats dusted and inspected for damage and breakage. The side windows, windshield and mirrors should be cleaned, along with lights and reflectors.

Weekly cleaning routine

Floors and seats should be washed. The exterior should be washed and the paint inspected. Door hinges and operating mechanisms should be oiled and checked.

VI. SCHOOL-BUS ROUTES

The owner and driver of a school bus should be thoroughly familiar with the area. When route layouts are considered, the driver should help make recommendations to the school board, parents and, where applicable, the vehicle owner. A well-planned route can be the safest. Information on the route should be available to everyone affected by the service.

Consider these factors when laying out routes and planning schedules:

- Age, health and physical condition of the passengers
- Condition of the roads to be travelled
- School schedule
- Distances between homes and school
- Distances between homes and routes
- Safety of walking routes between homes and routes
- Number and size of available buses
- Number of passengers to be served
- Size of area
- Location of bus stops
- Seasonal conditions (such as snow banks)
- Location of safe turnaround points

In choosing a route:

- Examine bad curves, steep hills, rough roads, narrow bridges, railroad crossings and other hazards. Avoid these whenever possible.
- Make sure bus stops are free from physical hazards.
- Route buses as near to the homes of passengers as traffic, time and convenience permit.

- Where possible, pick up and drop off passengers on the home side of the road, to eliminate or reduce the number of passengers forced to cross the road.
- Prepare and follow a time schedule.
- Make sure turnaround points are safe in all weather, with firm traction and good visibility of oncoming traffic.

Chapter 5-Summary

By the end of this chapter, you should know:
- How to load and unload passengers
- The stopping-for-school-buses law and to whom it applies
- Special precautions for school buses
- Emergency procedures and evacuation process
- School bus daily care and maintenance
- Planning and designing a school-bus route

CHAPTER 6
KEEPING YOUR LICENCE

Ontario has a one-piece driver's licence. The licence card has a photograph and signature of the driver. All drivers in Ontario should have a one-piece licence card. You must carry your licence with you whenever you drive.

Renewing your licence

When your licence is due for renewal, you will get a renewal application form in the mail. At this time, you will be provided with information about the requirements to renew your licence, which may include any combination of vision, written and road tests, in addition to submitting a medical report.

If any tests are required, you must complete the tests at a DriveTest Centre prior to renewal. If no tests are required, you must renew your licence in person at a ServiceOntario centre. Take the form into any ServiceOntario centre in the province. They

are all equipped to take photographs. You will be asked to sign the form, show identification, pay a fee and have your photograph taken. You will get a temporary licence on the spot if your application and documents are in order, and your permanent one will be mailed to you. You must carry it with you whenever you drive and produce it when a police officer requests it.

If you do not get a renewal application form in the mail when your licence is due for renewal, call the Ministry of Transportation. You are responsible for making sure you have a valid driver's licence.

If your licence has been suspended, cancelled or expired for more than three years, you will

be required to re-apply for a licence in Ontario and meet all the requirements of graduated licensing, including passing all the required tests. Only then will you be eligible to re-apply for any commercial-class licences.

Medical reporting

If you have any commercial vehicle driver's licence other than a class D licence, you must pass a medical examination every one to five years, depending on your age. You will get a notice and a blank medical-report form in the mail three months before your medical report is due. You must go to a doctor and get a medical examination. The doctor completes the form. You must submit the form to the Ministry of Transportation, either by mail or in person. If you do not file a medical report, your class of licence will be downgraded.

- Drivers under the age of 46 are required to submit a medical report every five years.
- Drivers aged 46 to 64 are required to submit a medical report every three years.
- Drivers aged 65 or older are required to submit a medical report every year.

Changing your name or address

You must tell the Ministry of Transportation within six days of changing your name or address.

You will need a new licence when you change your address. You can change your address on the ServiceOntario website at www.serviceontario.ca, or at a ServiceOntario centre, or mail it to the Ministry of Transportation, P.O. Box 9200, Kingston, ON K7L 5K4. The ministry will send you a new licence.

Reason For Name Change	Documentation Required
Marriage	Government Issued Marriage Certificate Change-of-Name Certificate
Common Law Alliance	Change-of-Name Certificate
Adoption	Court Order for Adoption Change-of-Name Certificate
Under the *Change of Name Act*	Change-of-Name Certificate

When you get it, destroy your old licence and carry the new one.

If you change your name, you need a new licence. Take the documents you must show and your current licence to a ServiceOntario centre. A new photograph will be taken. You will get a temporary licence to use until your permanent licence is mailed to you. Carry it with you whenever you drive.

There is no charge for getting a new licence because you change your name or address.

The chart on the previous page shows the documents you will need to change your name on your driver's licence.

Driver's licence laws
It is illegal to:
- Lend your licence
- Let someone else use it
- Use an altered licence
- Use another licence as your own
- Have more than one Ontario driver's licence
- Use a fictitious or imitation licence

THE DEMERIT-POINT SYSTEM

The demerit-point system encourages drivers to improve their behaviour and protects people from drivers who abuse the privilege of driving. Drivers convicted of driving-related offences have demerit points recorded on their records. Demerit points stay on your record for two years from the date of the offence. If you accumulate too many demerit points, your driver's licence can be suspended.

Note: Class B and E licence holders may have no more than eight demerit points. A class B/E licence holder who exceeds eight demerit points will be automatically downgraded to the next-highest class for which they are eligible (for example, usually class C or F until their demerit points fall below eight).

OTHER WAYS TO LOSE YOUR LICENCE

Your licence may also be suspended for the following reasons:

Medical suspension

By law, all doctors must report the names and addresses of everyone 16 years or older who has any condition that may affect their ability to drive safely (for example, a stroke, heart condition or dizziness). Doctors report this information to the Ministry of Transportation, and it is not given to anyone else. Your driver's licence may be suspended until new medical evidence shows that the condition does not pose a safety risk.

Zero tolerance for commercial drivers

Drivers of commercial vehicles must not have any presence of alcohol and/or a drug in their system when driving a commercial vehicle. If a commercial driver has alcohol or a drug in their system, they will face serious penalties, including licence suspensions and administrative monetary penalties.

Commercial vehicle drivers (classes A to F) have a zero-tolerance sanction for drugs and alcohol impairment when behind the wheel of these types of vehicles:

- Those that require a class A-F licence
- One requiring a Commercial Vehicle Operator's Registration (CVOR)
- Road-building machine.

If police determine that you have the presence of drugs or alcohol in your system and/or that you are impaired by any substance including illegal drugs, prescription drugs or over-the-counter medications, you will face severe consequences, including potential criminal charges and jail time.

Impaired driving

Driving when your ability is impaired by alcohol or a drug, is a crime in Canada. Your vehicle does not even have to be moving; you can be charged if you are impaired behind the wheel, even if you have not started to drive. In circumstances involving possible impairment by a drug or a combination of alcohol and a drug, police can require a driver to:

- provide breath samples
- perform standardized field sobriety tests
- conduct a drug recognition evaluation
- provide oral fluid urine, or blood samples for screening

If you fail or refuse to comply with any of these demands, you will be charged under the Criminal Code.

If you are 21 years of age and under, you must not drive if you have been drinking alcohol. Your blood alcohol level must be zero.

For more information on impaired driving measures in Ontario, please visit the Ministry of Transportation website at: www.mto.gov.on.ca/english/safety/ impaired-driving.shtml

Alcohol

The police can stop any driver to determine if alcohol or drug testing is required. They may also do roadside spot checks. When stopped by the police, you may be told to blow into a machine that tests your breath for alcohol, a roadside screening device, or perform physical co-ordination tests. If you fail, are unable or refuse to provide a breath sample or to perform the physical co-ordination tests, you will be charged under the Criminal Code.

If you cannot give a breath sample or it is impractical to obtain a sample of breath, the police officer can require you to provide a blood sample instead.

Drugs

The police can stop any driver to determine if drug testing is required. Criminal Code and *HTA* sanctions apply to drivers impaired by alcohol or a drug.

Drugs in all forms, including cannabis, illegal drugs, prescription drugs or over-the-counter medications, can have dangerous effects:

- If you use prescription medicines or get allergy shots, ask your doctor about side effects such as dizziness, blurred vision, nausea or drowsiness that could affect your driving.
- Read the information on the package of any over-the-counter medicine you take. Any stimulant, diet pill, tranquillizer or sedative may affect your driving. Even allergy and cold remedies may have ingredients that could affect your driving.
- Drugs and alcohol together can have dangerous effects, even several days after you have taken the drug.

Do not take a chance; ask your doctor or pharmacist before you drive.

Chapter 6-Summary

By the end of this section, you should know:
- Your responsibility to maintain a valid driver's licence
- Common circumstances where your licence can be cancelled or suspended
- How alcohol and drugs affect your ability to drive
- The consequences that result from poor driving habits.

CHAPTER 7
ROAD TEST

As part of the Class B/E or C/F road test, you will be required

1. Through the Daily Inspection test, to determine the safe operation of the vehicle and identify any of the prescribed minor or major defects as listed in the applicable schedules in the Regulation. O. Reg. 199/07.

2. Through the Backing Skills test, to display backing skills essential for the safe control of the vehicle while reversing into a desired location and simultaneously judging the vehicle's position as it relates to surrounding objects.

3. Through the On-Road Driving test, to display skills required to drive a commercial vehicle in most traffic situations while obeying all relevant signs, signals and rules of the road.

The Class B/E or C/F road test is made up of the following components.

1. Daily inspection test:
- Exterior inspection
- In-cab check
- Interior inspection

2. Backing skills test:
- Offset backing–left or right, OR
- Alley dock (90-degree backing)

3. On-road driving test:
- Left and right turns
- Intersections
- Lane changes
- Driving along
- Expressway section
- Curves
- Roadside stop/start
- Loading and unloading (Class B/E)
- Railway crossing

Pre-test requirements

For a vehicle that is equipped with air brakes, you must bring the following:

- Wheel chocks or blocks
- Means of keeping time to measure seconds
- A means of holding the brake pedal in the applied position
- A device for measuring pushrod stroke

If you do not have all of the listed items, the road test will be declared out of order, and you must pay 50 per cent of the road-test fee before you may reschedule the test.

Note: Protective headgear/eyewear, a chart of brake-adjustment limits and a means of marking the pushrod (chalk or similar) are recommended items, but not mandatory.

Daily inspection report and applicable schedule

- Prior to the road test, you must provide the examiner with a valid and completed daily inspection report, as well as the applicable schedule relative to your vehicle.

Inspection stickers

- You must also ensure your vehicle has the appropriate annual inspection stickers or valid paper copies.
- Buses require an annual as well as a semi-annual inspection sticker.
- Semi-annual inspection sticker is required if the annual inspection sticker is older than six months.

DAILY INSPECTION TEST
Introduction and overview

The purpose of the daily inspection test is to determine if you have the knowledge and skills required for the safe operation of the vehicle and to identify any of the prescribed minor or major defects as listed in the applicable schedule(s) in the Ontario Regulation. O. Reg.199/07.

The daily inspection test is divided into the following sections and will be performed in the following order:

1. Exterior inspection
2. In-cab check
3. Interior inspection

The exterior and interior portions of the daily inspection test will be administered using a random selection of testing items from the applicable schedule in Regulation O. Reg. 199/07. This will ensure that you are prepared to inspect all components of the vehicle.

You will be required to inspect all items listed for the in-cab portion of the test. You will be permitted to use the applicable schedule as a guide and reference during the daily inspection test.

Exterior inspection

The exterior inspection of the vehicle must be performed with the parking brake engaged and the wheels chocked.

You will be asked to find and inspect four randomly generated items from the list below and be required to:
- Demonstrate and describe how you would inspect the particular item.
- Explain what the defect(s) would be for the particular item.
- Describe what action you would take upon identifying a minor and/or major defect.

For any road test where the vehicle is equipped with air brakes, you will be expected to be prepared to inspect any of the air brake components of the vehicle listed below as well as any of the other items listed below. The list below will also provide inspection methods for each item.

Exterior items:
1. Slow air pressure build-up rate
You must know the proper method for testing the air pressure build-up rate, and that a vehicle has this minor defect when it takes longer than two minutes for air pressure to build up from 85 to 100 psi.

Procedure:
- Ensure the trailer supply valve is closed (pulled out when equipped).
- Release the parking brake.
- Pump brakes to reduce air pressure to 552 kPa (80 psi or less).
- Maintain engine speed of 600 to 900 r.p.m.
- Note time for pressure to rise from 587 to 690 kPa (85 to 100 psi) while maintaining specified engine speed.
- Note the build-up time and tell the examiner.

2. Audible air leaks
You must know that it's necessary to check for leaks regularly, and a vehicle has this minor defect when any air leak can be heard.

Air-loss rate exceeds the prescribed limit
You must know the proper method for testing the air-loss rate, and that a vehicle has this major defect when the air pressure drops in one minute more than the prescribed limit of:
- 21 kPa (3 psi) in one minute

Procedure:
- Tell the examiner, "For any air leaks heard at any time, I would conduct the air-loss rate test."
- Ensure the vehicle is secured by wheel chocks.
- Release all spring parking/emergency brakes.
- Ensure the air-system pressure is between cut-in and cut-out values (80 -145 psi); shut off the engine and turn the key on (if required).
- Hold the brake pedal in the fully applied position.
- Observe the air pressure gauges for one minute and note any change. (Disregard the initial pressure drop and begin test after the pressure has stabilized.)

3. Pushrod stroke of any brake exceeds the adjustment limit

You must know the proper method for checking brake pushrod stroke, and that a vehicle has this major defect when the pushrod stroke of any brake is longer than the prescribed limit.

Certain vehicles do not provide access to measure the applied pushrod stroke (buses, low-slung vehicles and those with obstructive fairing or body panels, or vehicles equipped with air disk brakes). In such cases, the examination is conducted verbally.

Here are the steps you must take to measure applied pushrod stroke.

1. Secure the vehicle with wheel chocks or blocks.
2. Ensure air pressure is above 621 kPa (90 psi) and release the spring brakes.
3. Select one of the following methods:
   - **Method 1:** Mark the pushrod at the brake chamber or at a suitable fixed reference point. (Use chalk, soapstone, marker or other similar instrument. Marks must be narrow and precise.)
   - **Method 2:** Measure the released position of the pushrod. (Measure and note the distance from a point on the pushrod to a suitable fixed point at the brake chamber. This is measurement number 1.)
4. Raise or lower the air pressure by running the engine or pumping the brake pedal until both the primary and secondary air-tank gauges display 621 to 690 kPa (90 to 100 psi).
5. Shut off the engine.
6. Press and hold the brake pedal in the fully applied position.
7. Determine the applied pushrod stroke. (Continue to use the previously selected method.)
   - **Method 1:** Measure the distance from the brake chamber or fixed reference point to the mark on the pushrod.
   - **Method 2:** Measure the applied position of the pushrod. (Remeasure and note the distance from the previously selected point on the pushrod to the previously selected fixed point at the brake chamber. This is measurement number 2.) Subtract measurement 1 from measurement 2 to calculate the applied pushrod stroke measurement.
8. Determine and indicate the number size (such as 16, 20, 24 or 30) and type (such as standard or long-stroke) of the brake chamber.
9. Determine and indicate the adjustment limit for the brake chamber.
10. Compare the applied pushrod stroke to the applicable adjustment limit and identify any brake that exceeds the adjustment limit as defective.

4. Low-air warning system fails or system is activated

You must know the proper method for testing the low-air warning, and that a vehicle has this major defect when the low air-warning fails to activate or activates before air pressure drops below 55 psi.

Procedure:

- Ensure air pressure is above 621 kPa (90 psi). If air pressure is too low, warning may activate as soon as ignition key is turned on.
- Ensure ignition key is turned on. Engine may be running or shut off (If ignition key is not turned on, the warning will not activate)
- Press and release the brake pedal (to lower pressure) several times until warning activates.
- Watch the pressure gauges and note the pressure when the low-air warning device activates (Low-air warning device may be only a light, or a light and an audible device.)

5. Exhaust system-ALL

Exhaust leak

You must know how to visually inspect the exhaust system, and that a vehicle has this minor defect when there's a noticeable exhaust leak.

Exhaust leak that causes exhaust gas to enter the occupant compartment

You must know the hazard of prolonged exposure to engine exhaust gases, and that vehicle has this major defect when exhaust gases from an exhaust-system leak are getting into the cab.

Procedure:

- With the vehicle running, open the hood or other compartments as required and inspect the complete exhaust system to ensure there are no signs of exhaust leaks.

6. Glass and Mirrors-C/F

Required mirror or glass has broken or damaged attachments onto vehicle body

You must know that the windows and mirrors that are necessary for safe operation must also be securely attached to vehicle, and that the vehicle has this minor defect when the attachments for any required mirror or other glass are broken or damaged.

Procedure:

- Inspect the vehicle to ensure all external mirrors and mirror attachments onto the vehicle body are secure, not broken or damaged.

7. Hydraulic brake system-ALL

Brake fluid level is below indicated minimum level and brake fluid reservoir is less than one-quarter full

You must know the location of the hydraulic brake master-cylinder reservoir, how to check the level of the brake fluid, and that the vehicle has this minor defect when brake fluid level is below the mark indicating the minimum level as determined by the manufacturer, or a major defect when the reservoir is less than one-quarter full.

Brake fluid leak

You must know that brake fluid is required for the system to operate, that loss of brake fluid can cause the brakes to malfunction or fail completely, and that a vehicle has this major defect when there is a brake fluid leak.

Procedure:

Open the hood and inspect brake-fluid reservoirs to ensure:
- Brake fluid is above the minimum required level.
- There is no brake fluid leak.
- Brake-fluid reservoir is not less than one-quarter full.

8. Suspension system-ALL

Air leak in air-suspension system

You must know that a vehicle has a minor defect when an air leak is noticeable in the air-suspension system.

Damaged (patched, cut, bruised, cracked to in braid or deflated) air bag

You must know the normal appearance of air bags used in vehicle suspension systems, and be able to recognize the signs of damage and identify when the damage may also cause an air bag to be deflated. You must also know a vehicle has a major defect when any air bag is damaged and has no air in it.

Procedure:

- Inspect the vehicle (or describe the process) to ensure an air leak is not noticeable in the air-suspension system and any air bag is not damaged and has air in it.

9. Suspension system-ALL

Broken leaf spring

You must know the importance of doing a visual inspection of leaf springs, and how to identify broken leaf spring, and that a vehicle has this minor defect when any spring has a single broken leaf.

Cracked or broken main spring leaf or more than one broken leaf spring

You must know which leaves in a spring are considered to be "main" leaves, and that a vehicle has this major defect when either a main leaf or more than one other leaf is broken.

Part of leaf spring or suspension is missing, shifted out of place, in contact with another vehicle component

You must know the condition of the suspension-system components, and the hardware that attaches it to the vehicle need to be inspected visually; you must be able to recognize the signs of more serious unsafe suspension-system conditions, and that a vehicle has this major defect when any part of a leaf spring or suspension part is missing, has shifted out of place or is in contact with another vehicle component.

Broken spring on other than a leaf spring system (Class B/E only)
You must know the importance of doing a visual inspection of springs and how to identify a broken spring, and that vehicle has this major defect when any spring other than a leaf spring is broken.

Procedure:
• Inspect the vehicle (or describe the process where not accessible) to identify any cracked or broken springs, spring leaves, or a spring leaf or suspension part is missing, has shifted out of place or is in contact with another vehicle component.

10. Suspension system-ALL
Suspension fastener is loose, missing or broken
You must know the condition of the suspension-system components and the hardware that attaches it to the vehicle need to be inspected visually; you must be able to recognize the signs of loose, missing or broken components, and also know that a vehicle has this minor defect when any suspension fastener is loose, missing or broken.

Loose U-bolt
You must know how to locate and identify suspension U-bolts, know the importance of ensuring they remain tight and the signs of loose U-bolts. You must also know that a vehicle has this major defect when any spring U-bolt is loose.

Procedure:
• Inspect the condition of the suspension-system components and the hardware, including suspension fasteners and U-bolts, that attaches it to the vehicle for any visual signs of loose, missing or broken components.

11. Tires: Leaks-ALL
Tire leaking, if leak cannot be heard
You must know the importance of keeping tires properly inflated, appreciate the need to regularly check for leaks, and that a vehicle has this minor defect when a leak appears evident, but cannot be felt or heard in any tire.

Flat tire and tire leaking, if leak can be felt or heard
You must know the dangers of operating with a flat tire, and that a vehicle has this major defect when any tire is flat, or when a leak can be felt or heard.

Procedure:

- Select one tire of the vehicle and inspect it by listening and feeling for any leaks.

Note: Kicking the tires or using a mallet to check for flats is acceptable.

12. Tires: Damage and tread-ALL

Damaged tread or sidewall of tire

You must be able to distinguish between the tread and sidewall of a tire, and know the visual signs of tread and sidewall damage, and know that a vehicle has this minor defect when there is damage to the tread or sidewall area.

Tire tread depth is less than wear limit

You must know how to check tire-tread depth and the minimum allowable depth for various tire positions in vehicle safety regulations, and that a vehicle has this major defect when any tire's tread depth is below the allowable wear limit.

Tire is in contact with another tire or any vehicle component other than mud flap

You must know that tires should never contact other vehicle components, and while a tire contacting a mud flap is not a safety concern, a vehicle has this major defect when any tire is in contact with another tire or any other vehicle component.

Tire has exposed cords in the tread or outer sidewall area

You must know that tires are constructed with steel cords inside their casings, which are covered in rubber for protection, and that a vehicle has this major defect when cords are exposed in the tread or sidewall of any tire.

Procedure:

Select one tire of the vehicle and inspect it:

1. Damaged tread or sidewall of tire– (any visual signs such as cuts or other damage to treads and sidewalls)

2. Tire tread depth–to ensure the depth is greater than the minimum allowable depth for the tire positions in vehicle safety regulations (3mm steer tire and 1.5 mm for other tires)
3. Contact with another tire or any vehicle component other than mud flap-to ensure there is no contact
4. Exposed cords in the tread or outer sidewall area–to ensure there are no exposed cords in the tread or sidewall of any tire

13. Wheels, hubs and fasteners-ALL

Hub oil below minimum level (when fitted with sight glass)

You must know that wheel hubs use bearings that require lubrication, that oil is often used as a bearing lubricant, that hub caps used with oil-lubricated bearings may have a clear window allowing a visual inspection of the oil fill level, and that a vehicle has this minor defect when you can see that the hub-oil level is below minimum.

Leaking wheel seal
You must know that wheel hubs require seals to keep the lubricant inside the hub; when a wheel seal is leaking, the wheel bearing can fail, and that a vehicle has this minor defect when there is evidence of a leaking wheel seal.

Evidence of imminent wheel, hub or bearing failure
You must know the normal appearance of wheel and hub components, the visual indications of more serious unsafe conditions, and that a vehicle has this major defect when there is visual evidence that a wheel, hub or bearing failure could occur.

Procedure:

The examiner will select one wheel and require you to:
• Where sight glass is present (or describe the procedure if not present), inspect the hub-oil level to ensure oil is above the minimum level.

• Inspect to ensure there is no evidence of a leaking wheel seal–look inside the wheel for oil and stains.
• Inspect to ensure there is no visual evidence that a wheel, hub or bearing failure could occur.

14. Wheels, hubs and fasteners-ALL

Wheel has loose, missing or ineffective fastener
You must know the visual features of different types of wheel systems; the importance of keeping wheel fasteners (normally nuts and bolts) properly tightened; be able to detect missing fasteners and recognize the visual signs of loose or ineffective fasteners; and know that a vehicle has this major defect when any wheel has a loose, missing or ineffective fastener.

Evidence of imminent wheel, hub or bearing failure
You must know the normal appearance of wheel and hub components and the visual indications of more

serious unsafe conditions, and that a vehicle has this major defect when there is visual evidence that a wheel, hub or bearing failure could occur.

Procedure:
• Inspect for any missing fasteners and recognize the visual signs of loose or ineffective fasteners such as a gap between nut and wheel.
• Inspect to ensure there is no visual evidence that a wheel, hub or bearing failure could occur.

15. Wheels, hubs and fasteners-ALL

Damaged, cracked or broken wheel, rim, attaching part
You must know the visual features of different types of wheel systems, the normal appearance of the individual components, and that a vehicle has this major defect when any wheel, rim, or any part used to attach the wheel or rim, is damaged, cracked or broken.

Evidence of imminent wheel, hub or bearing failure
You must know the normal appearance of wheel and hub components and the visual indications of more serious unsafe conditions, and that a vehicle has this major defect when there is visual evidence that a wheel, hub or bearing failure could occur.

Procedure:
The examiner will select two wheel assemblies and require you to:
Inspect inner and outer wheel assembly (open hood if access will improve visibility) to ensure:
- Any wheel, rim, or any part used to attach the wheel or rim, is not damaged, cracked or broken.
- There is no visual evidence that a wheel, hub or bearing failure could occur.

16. Alternating overhead lamps-B/E
A lamp is missing or inoperative
You know which lamps on the bus are required, and that the bus has

this minor defect when any lamp is missing or inoperative. And that it is a major defect when the use of lamp is required, and any lamp is missing or inoperative.

Lamps do not alternate
You know which lamps on the bus alternate and that the bus has this minor defect when any lamp does not alternate. And that it is a major defect when the use of lamp is required and any lamp does not alternate.

A lamp is not of the proper colour
You know that the proper colour lamps on the bus are required, and that the bus has this minor defect when any lamp is not of the proper colour and a major defect when the use of lamp is required and a lamp is not of the proper colour.

Procedure:
- Activate alternating overhead lamps and ensure they function properly.

17. Doors and windows, other than emergency exits-B/E
A window or door fails to open or close securely
You must know that any window or door must be able to open and close securely, and that a vehicle has this minor defect when any window or door fails to open or close securely.

When carrying passengers, door fails to open or close securely
You must know that, when carrying passengers, a door must open and close as intended, and that a vehicle has this major defect when any door fails to work properly.

Procedure:
- Test the function of the window or door by opening and closing to ensure it opens and closes properly.

18. Emergency exits-ALL
Required alarm is inoperative
You must know how the required alarm functions, and that a vehicle

has this minor defect when the required alarm is inoperative and a major defect when carrying passengers and the required alarm is inoperative.

When carrying passengers:
- **Window fails to open from inside or close securely**
  You must know that, when carrying passengers, windows must be able to open and close securely, and that a vehicle has this major defect when windows fail to open or close securely.
- **Door fails to open freely from inside and outside**
  You must know that, when carrying passengers, a door must open and close as intended, and that a vehicle has this major defect when any door fails to work properly.

Procedure:
- Test the function of the window or door to ensure it opens and closes properly and the required alarm is operative.

19. Exterior body and frame-ALL

Insecure or missing body parts
You must know that secure vehicle body parts are necessary for safe operation, and the vehicle has this minor defect when any body parts are insecure or missing.

Insecure or missing compartment door
You must know that the compartment door is necessary for safe operation, and must be securely attached to the vehicle. And that the vehicle has this minor defect when the compartment door is insecure or missing.

Damaged frame or body
You must know that some conditions of the frame or cargo body can be serious safety concerns, and that a vehicle has this minor defect when it is visible that a frame or body is damaged.

One or more visibly shifted, cracked, collapsing or sagging frame member
You must know that some conditions of the frame or cargo body can be very serious safety concerns, and that a vehicle has this major defect when it is visible that any frame component has shifted, is cracked, collapsing or is sagging.

Procedure:
Inspect one side of the vehicle and open the hood (front-engine bus) to check for any:
- Insecure or missing body parts
- Insecure or missing compartment door
- Damaged frame or body
- One or more visibly shifted, cracked, collapsing or sagging frame member

20. Mirrors-B/E

Mirror has broken or damaged attachments onto vehicle body
You must know that the mirrors are necessary for safe operation, and must also be securely attached to vehicle body. And that the vehicle has this defect when the attachments for

any required mirror are broken or damaged.

A mirror is missing or broken
You must know that the mirrors are necessary for safe operation, and must also be securely attached to vehicle. And that the vehicle has this major defect when the required mirror is missing or broken.

The glass surface of a mirror has an aggregate non-reflective area exceeding 6.5 square centimeters
You must know the importance of the glass surface of a mirror, and that a vehicle has this major defect when the glass surface of a mirror has an aggregate non-reflective area exceeding 6.5 square centimeters.

Procedure:
Inspect vehicle to ensure:
• Any mirror attachment onto the vehicle body is not broken or damaged.

• A mirror is not missing or broken.
• The glass surface of any mirror does not have a non-reflective area of more than 6.5 square centimetres.

21. Pedestrian/student safety crossing arm-B/E
The arm is missing or fails to function as intended
You must know the student safety arm is securely mounted and functions properly, and that a vehicle has this minor defect when the arm is missing or fails to function as intended.

Procedure:
• Inspect vehicle to ensure that the student safety crossing arm is securely mounted and functions properly in conjunction with stop arm (gate).

22. Stop arm (if not equipped, must verbalize)-B/E
If equipped with flashing lamps to illuminate letters of the word "STOP," any lamp is partially or wholly inoperative:
• **Stop arm or stop sign is missing**
You must know when the stop arm or stop sign is required, and a vehicle has a minor defect when missing and a major defect when the stop arm or stop sign is required and missing.
• **Stop arm or stop sign is damaged so as to significantly affect visibility**
You must know when the stop arm or stop sign is required and a vehicle has a minor defect when damaged so significantly to affect visibility and a major defect when the stop arm or stop sign is required and damaged significantly affecting visibility.

- **Stop arm will not extend fully or stay fully extended**
  You must know how the stop arm functions, and the vehicle has a minor defect when it will not extend fully or stay fully extended, and a major defect when the stop arm or stop sign is required and will not extend fully or stay fully extended.

- **Either light on stop arm is inoperative, lights do not alternate or lights are not red**
  You must know when the light on the stop arm is required, and the vehicle has a minor defect when either light on the stop arm is inoperative, lights do not alternate or are not red, and a major defect when either light on the stop arm is required and is inoperative, lights do not alternate or are not red.

Diagram 7-1

Procedure:

Inspect the vehicle to ensure the stop arm:

- Lights function.
- Is mounted securely to the vehicle frame and is not damaged.
- Extends fully when operated.

In-cab check

Once the exterior inspection is complete, you will enter the vehicle and begin the in-cab check portion of the test, where you must point to or touch all items and fully explain what you are inspecting for each item. You are not required to list the minor or major defects.

During the in-cab check portion of the test you will be expected to start the vehicle and perform the following checks:

All the gauges	Confirm and indicate that all gauges and indicators are normal and working properly.
Air pressure gauge (air brake vehicle only)	Confirm and indicate air pressure gauge is working properly and is within normal operating range.
Driver's seat and seat belt	Confirm the driver seat is secure and seat belts are secure, and in good working condition.
Mirror and windshield	Check the windshield and confirm it is clear and has no obstructions or damage to the glass. Confirm the mirrors are properly adjusted.
Heater/defroster controls	Confirm the heater(s) and defroster(s) work in all positions.
Steering wheel	Confirm the steering wheel is securely attached to the vehicle, responds in the normal way and there is no excessive free play.
Wipers and washers	Confirm the windshield wipers and washer fluid are working normally.

Interior inspection

Once the in-cab check is complete, you will find and inspect two randomly generated items from the applicable Schedule and be required to:

- Demonstrate and describe how you would inspect the particular item.
- Explain what the defect(s) would be for the particular item.
- Describe what action you would take upon identifying a minor and/or major defect.

1. Driver seat-C/F

Seat is damaged or fails to remain in set position

You must know that the driver seat must be properly positioned to be able to control the vehicle, know the methods for confirming the seating positions, as well as the locking methods, and that the vehicle has this minor defect when the seat is damaged or won't stay in the position needed to drive.

Seat belt or tether belt is insecure, missing or malfunctions

You must know the importance of seat belts, how to properly wear them and the condition they must be in to function properly. You must know that a vehicle has this major defect when any seat belt or tether belt is insecure, missing or malfunctions.

Procedure:

Inspect:

- Driver seat to ensure it is not damaged and will stay in the position needed to drive.
- Seat belt to ensure tether belt is secure and works correctly clipped and unclipped.

2. Emergency equipment and safety devices-C/F

Emergency equipment is missing, damaged or defective

You must know what emergency equipment is required for the type of transport you are involved in, how to check it, and that a vehicle has this minor defect when any necessary emergency equipment is missing, damaged or doesn't work properly.

Procedure:

- Verbally identify where the emergency flares, lamp or reflectors are located and that they are working properly and secure.

3. Heater/defroster-ALL

Control or system failure

You must know the importance of the heater/defroster always being available for keeping the windshield clear of condensation, and that a vehicle has this minor defect when the heater/defroster system operates incorrectly.

Procedure:

- Turn on heater/defroster fan for all directional controls/positions and ensure the system operates correctly in all positions.

- When applicable, ensure the defroster keeps the windshield clear.

4. Glass and mirrors-C/F
Required mirror or window glass fails to provide the required view to the driver as a result of being cracked, broken, damaged, missing or maladjusted
You must know the importance of always having a clear view of the conditions around the vehicle, the windows and mirrors that are required on the vehicle, and that a vehicle has this minor defect when there's mirror- or window-glass damage that reduces this needed visibility.

Procedure:
- Inspect mirrors and windows for any cracks or damage that reduce the required view to the driver, and ensure mirrors are properly adjusted.

5. Windshield wiper/washer
Class C/F:
- **Wiper blade damaged, missing or fails to adequately clear driver's field of vision**
  You must know the normal condition and function of wiper blades, and be able to recognize when they no longer function well, and that a vehicle has this minor defect when a wiper blade is damaged, missing or won't clear the area of the windshield in front of the driver.
- **Control or system malfunction**
  You must know how to operate the windshield wipers and washers, know that ensuring they are available at all times requires periodic testing, and that a vehicle has this minor defect when the control or any part of the system fails to function properly.

- **When use of wipers or washer is required: wiper or washer fails to adequately clear driver's field of vision in area swept by driver's side wiper**
  You must know that being able to see the roadway clearly in poor weather is very important, that this visibility is dependent on the wipers being able to clear water, snow and ice from the windshield, and that a vehicle has this major defect when the prevailing weather conditions require use of the wipers or washers, and they are not able to keep clear the area swept by the driver's side wiper.

Class B/E:
- Control or system malfunction–minor or major when use of wipers or washer is required
- Wiper blade damaged, missing or fails to adequately clear driver's field of vision–minor or major when use of wipers or washer is required

- Wiper or washer fails to adequately clear the windshield in the areas swept by both wipers—minor or major when use of wipers or washer is required

Procedure:

Inspect vehicle to ensure:
- The windshield wipers and washers function properly in all directions.
- Any wiper blade is not damaged or missing, and will clear the windshield.

6. Passenger Compartment

Class B/E and C/F:
- **Stanchion padding is damaged**
  You know how to inspect the stanchion padding, and that the vehicle has this minor defect when the stanchion padding is damaged.
- **Damaged steps or floor**
  You know how to inspect the steps and floor, and that the vehicle has

this minor defect when they are damaged.
- **Insecure or damaged overhead luggage rack or compartment**
  You know how to inspect the overhead luggage rack or compartment, and that the vehicle has this minor defect when the overhead luggage rack or compartment is insecure or damaged.

Class C/F:
- **Malfunction or absence of required passenger- or mobility-device restraints**
  You know how to inspect the required passenger- or mobility-device restraints, and that the vehicle has this minor defect when they malfunction or are missing; and that it is a major defect when the affected position is occupied and the required passenger- or mobility-device restraints malfunction or are missing.

- **Passenger seat is insecure**
  You know how to inspect the passenger seat, and that the vehicle has this minor defect when it is insecure; and that it is a major defect when the passenger seat is occupied and the seat is insecure.

Procedure:

Inspect passenger compartment and seat to ensure:
- Stanchion padding is not damaged.
- Steps or floor are not damaged.
- Overhead luggage rack or compartments are secure and not damaged.

Class C/F:
- Required passenger- or mobility-device restraints function properly.
- Passenger seat is secure.

7. Emergency equipment and safety devices-B/E

Emergency flares, lamps or reflectors:

- **Missing or insecure**
  You know what emergency equipment is required for the vehicle, how to check it, and that a vehicle has this minor defect when any emergency flares, lamps or reflectors are missing, damaged or don't work properly.

Fire extinguisher:

- **Fire extinguisher is missing**
  You know that a fire extinguisher is required, how to inspect it, and that the vehicle has this minor defect when the fire extinguisher is missing, and that it is a major defect when missing and carrying passengers.

- **The gauge on any required fire extinguisher indicates an empty condition or a complete lack of pressure**
  You know how to inspect a fire-extinguisher gauge, and that the vehicle has this minor defect when the gauge indicates an empty condition or a complete lack of pressure; and that it is a major defect when the gauge on any required fire extinguisher indicates an empty condition or a complete lack of pressure when carrying passengers.

- **Fire extinguisher is not securely mounted or stored in a manner that prevents the extinguisher from being a projectile object**
  You know when a fire extinguisher is securely mounted, and that the vehicle has a minor defect when the fire extinguisher is not securely mounted or stored in a manner that prevents the extinguisher from being a projectile object.

First aid kit:

- **Required first aid kit is missing**
  You know where the required first aid kit is located, and that the vehicle has this minor defect when the required first aid kit is missing, and that it is a major defect when carrying passengers and the required first aid kit is missing.

- **Kit is incomplete**
  You know where the required first aid kit is located, and that the vehicle has this minor defect when the kit is incomplete.

Procedure:

Identify where the emergency equipment and safety devices listed below are located, and describe that they are working properly and secure:

- Emergency flares, lamp or reflectors
- Fire extinguisher
- First aid kit

8. Seat and seat belt-B/E

Driver's seat fails to remain in set position

You must know that the driver seat must be properly positioned to be able to control the vehicle, and know the methods for confirming the seating positions, as well as the locking methods; and that the vehicle has this minor defect when the seat won't stay in the set position needed to drive.

Restraint system for passenger in mobility device or mobility-device restrain system, or component of either system, is missing or defective
You know how to inspect the restraint system for a passenger in a mobility device or mobility-device restrain system, and that the vehicle has this minor defect when the device is missing or defective.

Required restraint system or component of required restraint system is missing
You know how to inspect the required restraint system or component of it, and that the vehicle has this minor defect when the device is missing; and that it is a major defect when the affected position is occupied, and the required restraint system or component is missing.

Restraint system or component of restraint system is defective
You know how to inspect the restraint system or component of it, and that the vehicle has this minor defect when the device is defective; and that it is a major defect when affected position is occupied, and the restraint system or component is defective.

Seat is insecure
You must know how to inspect the driver seat, and that the vehicle has this minor defect when the seat is insecure; and that it is a major defect when affected position is occupied, and the seat is insecure.

Passenger restraint system, mobility-device restraint system, or component of either system, is missing or defective
You know how to inspect the passenger restraint system, and that the vehicle has this major defect if the system is missing or defective when the affected position is occupied.

Passenger seat or passenger-protection barrier is insecure
You must know how to inspect the passenger-protection barrier, and that the vehicle has this major defect when affected position, or position behind, is occupied and passenger seat or passenger-protection barrier is insecure.

Seat back or passenger-protection barrier padding is missing, partially missing or has shifted from position so as not to be effective
You must know how to inspect the seat back or passenger-protection barrier padding, and that the vehicle has this major defect when affected position, or position behind, is occupied, and seat back and passenger or passenger-protection barrier padding is missing, partially missing or has shifted from position as not to be effective.

9. Doors and emergency exits-C/F

Door, window or hatch fails to open or close securely

You must know that any window, door or hatch must be able to be opened and closed securely, and that a vehicle has this defect when any window or door fails to open or close securely.

Procedure:

• Test the function of the window or door by opening and closing to ensure it opens and closes properly.

BACKING SKILLS TEST

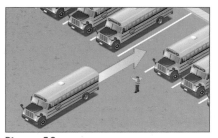

Diagram 7-2

Introduction

The purpose of the backing skills test is to test basic backing skills essential for the safe control of the vehicle while reversing into a desired location, and simultaneously judging the vehicle's position as it relates to surrounding objects during the exercise.

Examiners will be outside of the vehicle, always visible to you but will not coach or guide you as you are backing.

Required backing manoeuvres

You will be required to perform one backing manoeuvre during the test, either a 90-degree alley dock (driver's side), offset left or offset right.

Cones will be used to mark the boundaries for each manoeuvre; you must not hit any of the cones; and your vehicle should be as straight as possible within the cones when complete. You must secure the vehicle and inform the examiner you are finished.

For proper backing procedure refer to page 32 on backing. During the road test, you will be scored on the following:

• **Observation**–Before backing, you must exit the vehicle to check its path and observe the environment around the vehicle; and while backing, you must use mirrors to check the vehicle path.
• **Signals/Horn**–You must activate the four-way flashers and sound the electric horn before backing.
• **Speed**–Always reverse at a walking pace.
• **Pull-Ups**–When you stop and pull forward to get a better position, it is scored as a "pull-up." Stopping without changing direction does not count as a pull-up. You will not be penalized for initial pull-ups. However, an excessive number of pull-ups will count as errors.
• **Final Position**–You must back the vehicle as close as possible to the final position.

ON-ROAD DRIVING TEST

You will drive over a test route that has a variety of traffic situations. At all times during the test, you must drive in a safe and responsible manner; and wear your safety belt. Obey all traffic signs, signals, and laws. Complete the test without an accident or moving violation. During the driving test, the examiner will be scoring you on specific driving manoeuvres, as well as on your general driving behavior. You will follow the directions of the examiner. Directions will be given to you so that you will have plenty of time to do what the examiner has asked. You will not be asked to drive in an unsafe manner. If your test route does not have certain traffic situations, you may be asked to simulate a traffic situation. You will do this by telling the examiner what you would do if you were in that traffic situation.

As part of the road test, you will be expected to drive in a variety of traffic situations including:
- Left and right turns
- Intersections
- Lane changes
- Driving along
- Curves
- Expressway section
- Roadside stop/start
- Loading and unloading (Class B/E)
- Railway crossing

I. LEFT AND RIGHT TURNS

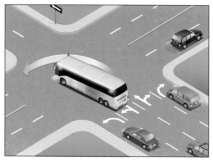

The approach

Traffic check
When approaching a turn you must monitor the surrounding traffic ahead. Conduct a visual search of the intersection for other vehicles, pedestrians, and objects.

Lane change
You must correctly select the lane(s) for entering the intersection. This may involve completing a lane change to get into the appropriate lane.

Signal
You must activate turn signals on approach as soon as appropriate.

Speed
You must gradually slow your vehicle to allow for proper control and to ensure smooth traffic flow.

Transmission/gears
You must select a gear that is ap-

propriate for the vehicle speed, and load that allows the engine to operate within its normal r.p.m. range.

Lane position

You must plan the correct pathway for entering and exiting the intersection.

If stopping

Smooth stop

You must be aware of traffic conditions and complete a smooth stop.

Full stop

Keep the vehicle under control while stopped. Do not roll backward or forward.

Stop position/gap

Stop in the proper legal stop position to see the area ahead. Stopping with reasonable space between your vehicle and the vehicle ahead allows you to be able to manoeuvre the vehicle if necessary. Move forward when adequate space becomes available ahead.

Wheels

Keep the wheels straight while waiting to turn. With curved sidewalks, the vehicle can be angled to follow the curb.

Traffic check

Monitor the surrounding traffic ahead. Before entering the intersection, you must check to the left, ahead, to the right and behind to ensure the way is clear.

Turning

Traffic check

Monitor the surrounding traffic ahead, beside and through the vehicle mirrors.

Both hands/gear

You must maintain a two-handed grip on the steering wheel as much as possible during an intersection crossing. Minimize gear changes during an intersection crossing and avoid all unnecessary gear changes. Any grade change in an intersection may also necessitate a gear change to maintain a consistent speed.

Speed/right-of-way

You must complete the turn at a speed appropriate for the conditions. You must recognize and correctly respond to right-of-way obligations in making the turn. Failure to take own right-of-way will impede traffic.

Wide/short

You must follow the path that is appropriate for your vehicle size and length. Do not travel too far away from the normal lane position, to avoid creating unnecessary space.

Complete turn

Traffic check

You must make regular traffic checks to be aware of the traffic patterns that flow around the vehicle (for example, ahead, sides and rear).

Correct lane

You must turn into the lane that corresponds to the lane you were in at the start of the turn. Turn into a lane that permits travel and acceleration without the added burden of attempting a lane change because of parked cars or other obstructions.

Signals/speed/gears

Signals must be cancelled so that other drivers do not get confused. Smooth, even acceleration prevents damage to the vehicle. It is important that the vehicle picks up speed and does not delay other traffic.

Moves right

Upon completion of a left turn, you must select the lane that provides the safest unimpeded travel for through traffic.

II. INTERSECTIONS

Stop intersections

The approach

Traffic check

While approaching the intersection, you must monitor the surrounding traffic ahead. Watch for signage, observe traffic-control devices and monitor traffic flow. Respond to potential obstructions or delays that can prevent travelling through the intersection at a normal rate.

Speed

Gradual slowing allows for proper control of the vehicle. To ensure smooth traffic flow and equipment/shipment integrity, you must be aware of traffic conditions and execute smooth manoeuvres.

Transmission/gears

You must select a gear that is appropriate for the vehicle speed and load that allows the engine to operate within its normal r.p.m. range.

Lane position

You must stay in the same lane approaching the intersection and not change position or lanes unnecessarily to ensure traffic flow is smooth and safe.

Stopping

Smooth stop

You must be aware of traffic conditions and execute smooth manoeuvres.

Full-stop roll

Making a full stop allows you enough time to thoroughly observe the traffic environment around the vehicle. You must keep the vehicle under control while stopped. Do not roll backward or forward.

Stop position/gap

Stopping in the proper legal stop position allows you to see the area ahead. Stopping in the intersection may impede the flow of cross traffic. Stopping with enough space between your vehicle and the vehicle ahead allows you to be able to manoeuvre the vehicle if necessary. You must move forward when adequate space becomes available ahead.

Traffic check

While waiting, you must monitor the surrounding traffic ahead, beside and in the vehicle mirrors to alert yourself to any changes in traffic conditions.

Starting

Traffic check

Before entering the intersection, you must monitor the surrounding traffic ahead.

Speed/right-of-way

You must start vehicle movement within a reasonable time when permitted by the traffic light and/or the movement of the vehicle ahead. You must also enter and travel through the intersection in a reasonable time.

Both hands/gears

You must maintain a two-handed grip on the steering wheel. Situations where only one hand is on the wheel must be limited to times when it is necessary to operate other vehicle controls or make a gear selection.

Lane position

You must follow the correct pathway upon entering and exiting the intersection. Do not change lanes or position in the intersection.

Traffic check

Keeping a constant visual search through the vehicle mirrors will alert you to any changes in condition.

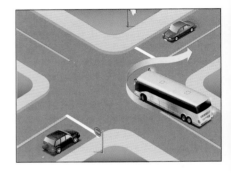

Through intersections

The approach

Traffic check

While approaching the intersection, you must monitor the surrounding traffic ahead.

Speed

Maintain speed approaching the intersection to ensure there is not a disruption in traffic flow. If there is any cross traffic that might enter the intersection ahead, you must slow down or cover the brake.

Gap
Safe following distance must be maintained and adjusted to allow for a safe stop.

Lane/position
You must stay in the same lane/position as you approach the intersection to ensure traffic flow is smooth and safe.

Driving through

Lane/position
You must stay in the same lane/position as you travel through the intersections to ensure traffic flow is smooth and safe.

Both hands/gears
To maintain proper control of the vehicle, your hands should be on the steering wheel. Any necessary

transmission shifts should be made prior to entering an intersection. Downshifting prior to an intersection may be necessary to avoid lugging the engine.

Traffic check
Checking mirrors after clearing an intersection allows you to be continually aware of conditions so that necessary adjustments in speed and position can be made.

III. LANE CHANGES

Traffic checks
In anticipation of making a lane change, you must observe traffic to identify where and when the lane change should be made.

Signal
You must signal to alert other motorists of the intention to change lanes. The signal can be initiated at any reasonable time before the lane change,

and must be cancelled when the lane change is complete.

Spacing
You must maintain a safe following distance within your current lane while preparing to make the lane change. The space you will require in the target lane must be adequate for the vehicle's length. You must check mirrors for vehicles traveling alongside, passing or approaching from the rear, and any vehicle that may already be in—or may enter—a blind spot.

Speed
You should operate within 10 km/h of the posted speed limit if conditions permit without exceeding the posted limit.

Changing lane
You must observe road and pavement markings. You must make the lane change at a point of the roadway where road conditions and mark-

ing indicate the lane change can be made. Intersections, pedestrian crossings, railway crossings and solid pavement markings are locations that are not suitable for making a lane change.

Lane change motion
The lane change itself needs to be deliberate, but smooth and steady. Sudden lateral movements should be avoided and taking too much time allows the traffic patterns to change during the lane change. Hesitating may also cause other motorists to change speed or position. The vehicle should be steered into the centre of the target lane adjusting speed as necessary to establish safe distances from other vehicles.

IV. DRIVING ALONG

Traffic check
Look well ahead as you drive; also, mirror checks are critical because of the vehicle's large blind spots. You must be continually aware of conditions so that necessary adjustments in speed and position can be made.

Speed
You should operate within 10 km/h of the posted speed limit if conditions permit without exceeding the posted limit.

Spacing
Because of the increased stopping distance of commercial vehicles, you must adjust the following distance to observe, react or manoeuvre the vehicle if necessary. You must also avoid driving beside or in the blind spot of other vehicles. You may need space to suddenly change lanes. When traffic is heavy, avoiding driving beside other vehicles may be difficult.

Lane usage
You should choose the right-most lane that can be travelled safely. Staying as far to the right as possible will minimize the disruption of traffic flow and keep hazards to the left side of the vehicle, where the view is less restricted.

Exiting

Traffic check
You must look ahead for exit signs and be aware of the proper lane to use for exiting, as well as checking ahead, behind, and to the side for traffic when preparing to exit safely.

Signal
The signal should be activated before slowing and while still on the expressway lane so other drivers can prepare or adjust their driving if required. The signal must also be cancelled.

Exit lane

If a lane change is required to move to the exit lane, the move must be deliberate, but smooth and steady.

Speed

You should not be slowing down on the expressway. The exit lane should be used to slow down.

Spacing

Because of the increased stopping distance of commercial vehicles, the following distance must be adjusted to allow you to observe, react or manoeuvre the vehicle if necessary.

V. CURVE

Speed

You must adjust speed to safely negotiate a curve. Drivers inexperienced with the operation of a particular type of vehicle often misjudge the maximum speed with which they can safely negotiate a curve of a given radius. Excessive speed prior to the curve often requires hard braking.

Lane position

Because of the off-tracking of large vehicles, you must approach the curve from an outside position of the lane to keep the rear wheels from cutting across the top of the curve. Failure to do so can cause the rear wheels to leave the road or present a hazard to vehicles in a neighboring lane.

Traffic check

A constant visual search around the vehicle is necessary to alert yourself to any changes in traffic. Mirror checks are critical because of the vehicle's large blind spots and off-tracking of rear wheels. You must be continually aware of conditions so that necessary adjustments in speed and position can be made. These adjustments take longer in commercial vehicles because of their large size; you must be able to anticipate them as early as possible.

VI. EXPRESSWAY

Entering

Traffic check

You must look ahead, in your mirrors and pay attention to the other vehicles on the expressway while accelerating on the on ramp to determine a safe opportunity to merge. It is important to remember the onus is on you–and not other vehicles–to merge safely onto the expressway.

Signal

The proper signal must be activated early, as soon as other vehicles can see you on the on-ramp and not cancelled until your vehicle is in the new lane to give other vehicles time to make any necessary adjustments. However, keep in mind that you do not have the right-of-way.

Spacing

Because of the increased stopping distance of loaded or empty trucks and other commercial vehicles, the following distance must be adjusted to allow you the ability to observe, react or manoeuvre the vehicle if necessary. You must also stay within the lane markings.

Speed

You should not exceed but travel as closely to the posted ramp advisory speed limit as possible. Use the acceleration lane to gain as much speed as necessary, and reach as closely to the expressway speed as possible.

Merge

The merge needs to be deliberate, but smooth and steady. Sudden lateral movements should be avoided. Taking too much time should also be avoided. The vehicle should be steered into the centre of the target lane while adjusting speed necessary to establish safe distances from other vehicles.

VII. ROADSIDE STOP/START

The approach

Traffic check

While approaching the stop, you must monitor the surrounding traffic ahead.

Speed/gears

Gradual slowing allows for proper control of the vehicle. You must select a gear that is appropriate for the vehicle speed and load that allows the engine to operate within its normal r.p.m. range.

Signal

Appropriate signals must be used to communicate with other road users, but not too early.

Lane/stop position

Stop as far to the right as possible to minimize disruption of traffic flow, and park so that the vehicle does not restrict vision or cause distractions to other vehicles. Vehicles must be parked parallel and close to the curb or edge of roadway without hitting the curb.

Stopping

Full-stop roll

Once you have reached the final parking position, you must secure the vehicle against movement. It is important that service brakes remain applied until the parking brake is activated.

Signals

The turn signal must be cancelled and the four-way flashers activated so as not to confuse other traffic.

Secure vehicle

For the safety of all around the vehicle, it is important to secure the vehicle against any movement.

Starting

Start

To move the vehicle safely, you must place it in the correct gear and not attempt to pull forward without releasing the brake.

Signals

Cancel the four-way flashers and activate the left-turn signal to warn traffic of the intention to enter the lane. The left-turn signal must be cancelled as soon as you have entered the driving lane.

Traffic check

Observe the traffic environment ahead, left and right, and check mirrors so that you will be alerted to any changes around the vehicle, with checks especially in the direction of the merge.

Speed/gears

Accelerating and merging properly prevents the vehicle from interfering with traffic flow.

Traffic check

Once you have resumed traffic speed, make sure to check the mirrors to be aware of the traffic environment.

VIII. LOADING AND UNLOADING

The approach

Traffic check

While approaching the stop, you must monitor the surrounding traffic ahead, beside and to the rear through the vehicle mirrors to ensure the location is safe, and a safe stop can be made.

Signal

Appropriate signals must be used to communicate with other road users to make sure that all are warned that a school bus is about to stop, and children are being loaded or unloaded.

Speed

Gradual slowing allows for proper control of the vehicle. To ensure smooth traffic flow and safety of students, you must be aware of traffic conditions and execute smooth manoeuvres.

Stopping

Stop position

You must maintain lane position to ensure the safety of the students, and ensure that other traffic does not attempt to pass the bus.

Secure vehicle

You must make sure that the bus cannot move while children are boarding or getting off, or before the children completely clear the area. You must also make sure that all traffic is warned that a stopped school bus is present, with children getting on or off.

Loading and unloading

Traffic check

A constant visual search around the vehicle will alert you to any changes in conditions. You must look for any vehicle movement around the bus and must ensure that all traffic in the area has come to a full stop.

Stop arm/gate

To ensure that all traffic is warned that a stopped school bus is present and children are getting on or off.

Door

You must see each student after they have left the bus, and that those leaving the bus have safely crossed the road or highway and have reached a safe area or safe distance from the vehicle. Every student should be seen clear of the bus area. When they get on, you should see that each student is seated safely.

Resume

Traffic check

Conduct a visual search for traffic/hazards around the school bus to ensure the area is safe for you to proceed.

Convex mirror check
Check for traffic/hazards around the school bus to ensure the area is safe for you to proceed.

Speed/gears
Accelerating properly prevents the vehicle from interfering with traffic flow. Accelerating too quickly may injure students in the bus, or may also cause the vehicle to stall or break down.

Cancel signal
Four-way flashers need to be manually cancelled so other road users are not confused.

IX. RAILWAY CROSSING
The approach

Traffic check
While approaching the railway crossing, you must monitor the surrounding traffic ahead, beside and to the rear through the vehicle mirrors to ensure the location is safe.

Speed/gears
Gradual slowing allows for proper control of the vehicle. To ensure smooth traffic flow and equipment/shipment integrity, you must be aware of traffic conditions and execute smooth manoeuvres.

Signal
Appropriate signals must be used to communicate with other road users, but not so early as to confuse traffic that may be exiting driveways or entering other intersections.

Lane/stop position
Stopping in the right-most lane would minimize disruption of traffic flow.

Stopping

Full-stop roll
Once you stop, you must ensure the vehicle doesn't roll forward or backward.

Stop position
At a controlled railway crossing, five metres from the nearest rail may be too close to stop, because in rare situations, the stop arm may hit the vehicle.

Traffic check
You must observe along the railway track to ensure there are no trains approaching.

Door

Opening the door will assist you in listening for any trains that may be approaching.

Starting

Traffic check

Observe the traffic environment ahead, left and also right; check mirrors so that you will be alerted to any changes around the vehicle to ensure that the rail tracks are clear, and there is enough clearance at the other side of the tracks.

Door

For safety reasons, doors must be closed prior to moving the vehicle.

Speed

Accelerating properly prevents the vehicle from interfering with traffic flow. Accelerating too quickly may damage equipment or injure passengers, which may in turn cause the vehicle to stall or break down.

Both hands/gears

You must maintain a two-handed grip on the steering wheel as much as possible during a railway crossing. You must not change gears while crossing a railway, and must select a gear that will not require changing while crossing.

Lane position

You must stay in the same lane approaching and travelling through the railway crossing to ensure traffic flow is smooth and safe.

Traffic check

Checking mirrors after clearing a railway allows you to be continually aware of conditions so that necessary adjustments in speed and position can be made.

Cancel signal

The signal must be cancelled so that other road users are not confused.

You will also be scored on your overall performance in the following categories:

Observation

You must be continually aware of conditions so that necessary adjustments in speed and position can be made. It is important to constantly monitor mirrors to see vehicles approaching and observe where the vehicle is tracking.

Intersection/railway traffic check

While travelling up to the intersection or railway crossing, you must monitor the surrounding traffic ahead, beside and to the rear through the vehicle mirrors.

Lane usage

If you observe the environment ahead, you should choose the rightmost lane that can be travelled safely. Stay as far to the right as possible. You may also use the next lane if the right-most lane requires constantly changing lanes.

Speed

You should operate within 10 km/h of the posted speed limit if conditions permit without exceeding the posted limit.

Spacing

Following distance must be adjusted to allow you to observe, react or manoeuvre the vehicle if necessary. You must also avoid passing too closely.

Clutch/gears

Proper use of the clutch eliminates unnecessary stress on the drivetrain, which can lead to equipment damage or breakdowns.

Brakes/accelerator

To ensure smooth traffic flow and equipment/shipment integrity, you must be aware of traffic conditions and execute smooth manoeuvres.

Gradual slowing also allows proper control of the vehicle.

Steering

Keeping both hands on the wheel is better to be able to control the vehicle during quick evasive manoeuvres. You must maintain a two-handed grip on the steering wheel as much as possible. Situations where only one hand is on the wheel must be limited to times when it is necessary to operate other vehicle controls or make a gear selection.

Turn signals

Signals alert other traffic that you are about to merge, exit or change lanes. Turn signals on most commercial vehicles are not self-cancelling and need to be manually cancelled so other road users are not confused.

CHAPTER 8
ADDITIONAL INFORMATION

I. ONTARIO'S DRIVE CLEAN PROGRAM

Vehicles powered by gasoline and diesel give off air pollutants and gases such as oxides of carbon, nitrogen and sulphur, hydrocarbons and soot. These pollutants affect the quality of the air we breathe, our health, crop yields and even the global climate.

Hydrocarbons and oxides of nitrogen react in sunlight to form ground-level ozone, better known as smog. Smog is a major health hazard responsible for respiratory ailments and other illnesses.

Oxides of sulphur and nitrogen combine with water vapour to form acid rain, which damages our lakes, forests and crops.

Global warming is the result of too much carbon dioxide and other gases trapping heat in our atmosphere. Global warming could cause average temperatures to rise, causing droughts, crop failures, lower water levels and more frequent and severe storms.

Vehicles are the single, largest domestic source of smog-causing emissions in Ontario. Drive Clean, administered by the Ministry of the Environment, reduces smog-causing pollutants by identifying grossly polluting vehicles and requiring them to be repaired.

If you own a light-duty vehicle in the Drive Clean Program area (southern Ontario from Windsor to Ottawa) that is five years old or older and is a 1988 or newer model, you must take your vehicle for a Drive Clean test every two years in order to renew its registration. Light-duty vehicles manufactured before the 1988 model year are exempt from Drive Clean emissions-test requirements. If you are buying a

used vehicle that is older than the current model year and is a 1988 or newer model, the vehicle must pass a Drive Clean test to transfer the ownership and plate it for the road.

Ontario requires all diesel-powered, heavy-duty trucks and buses province-wide to pass an annual Drive Clean emissions test. All non-diesel, heavy-duty vehicles require annual tests if they are registered in the designated Drive Clean light-duty vehicle program area.

You don't have to wait for a Drive Clean test to do something positive for the environment. Keeping your vehicle well maintained according to the manufacturer's recommended service schedules is an important part of driving clean. For example, if the "check engine" or "service engine" lights come on, have your engine looked at by a qualified repair technician as soon as possible. Otherwise, you could face costly repairs to the vehicle's engine or emissions-control system.

Please note that the act of creating, distributing or using false Drive Clean passes is an offence under the *Environmental Protection Act*. Emissions inspectors who do so can be decertified; vehicle owners will be charged.

For more information on Ontario's Drive Clean program, visit www.driveclean.com or call the Drive Clean Call Centre toll-free at 1-888-758-2999.

II. HIGH OCCUPANCY VEHICLE (HOV) LANES

A High Occupancy Vehicle (HOV) lane is a specially designed lane that is designated for use by certain types of vehicles with a specified number of occupants. It can offer travel-time savings to those who choose to carpool or take transit. HOV lanes can move a greater number of people than a general traffic lane, and encourage carpooling and transit use by providing travel-time savings and a more reliable trip time. HOV lanes are open 24 hours a day, seven days a week.

HOV lanes benefit all drivers, not only those who carpool, in the following ways:

- Improves highway infrastructure by moving more people in fewer cars
- Reduces the number of vehicles on the road
- Reduces vehicle emissions and improves air quality
- Helps you conserve fuel, save money (by sharing the cost of driving) and reduce stress

HOV lanes on provincial highways are reserved for vehicles carrying at least two people (for example, a driver plus at least one passenger in any of the following passenger vehicles: cars, minivans, motorcycles, pickup trucks, taxis, buses and limousines).

The HOV lane is separated from the other general traffic lanes by a striped buffer zone. It is illegal and unsafe to cross the striped buffer pavement markings.

Certain vehicles are exempt from the HOV lane rules. Buses can use an HOV lane at any time, regardless of the number of occupants. Emergency vehicles such as police, fire and ambulance are also exempt from the restrictions.

If you use the HOV lanes improperly, you can be stopped and ticketed by a police officer. You will be required to re-enter the general lanes at the next entry/exit zone.

III. DRIVING EFFICIENTLY

Smart driving practices

Fuel efficiency starts when you turn on your engine. Proper warm-up helps lubricate components and seals, reducing wear and leakage. Starting your bus properly can save money on fuel. As a driver, you can help to protect the environment from the harmful effects of driving by following these suggestions:

- When starting your vehicle, make sure you use zero throttle and are in a gear that doesn't need any.
- Don't pump the throttle unnecessarily; the amount of fuel required for starting is pre-measured, so it is wasteful and can damage cylinder walls.
- Use ether sparingly when having difficulty starting your engine; excessive use can harm the engine.
- Let your vehicle warm up for three to five minutes–if the temperature is below 0 degrees Celsius, allow it to warm up for seven to 10 minutes. Do not rev the engine; let it warm up gradually.
- Warm up your vehicle after the initial idle time by driving easily; don't try to get too much speed out of the engine by pushing the throttle down hard.
- Ensure oil and air pressure are in their normal operating ranges during start-up.
- Back off the accelerator when going down a hill, and let gravity and momentum do the work.
- Use cruise control where appropriate.
- Change gears smoothly–shifting professionally will result in about 30 per cent improvement in operating costs.
- Always use the clutch; failure to do so can wear down the gear teeth in the transmission.
- Practise progressive gear shifting at approximately 1600 r.p.m. Shifting before you reach the maximum governed r.p.m. reduces equipment wear, decreases noise levels and saves fuel.

- Run the engine in the highest gear range to keep it in low revs.
- Use your retarder properly, and turn it off when you don't need it. Allow the terrain to work for you.
- Turn off your engine when you stop for any length of time. You will save fuel, reduce maintenance requirements, prolong engine life and prevent unnecessary emissions.

Fuel-consumption techniques summary

If you learn and practise the following techniques, you will be well on the way to good fuel consumption:

- Use good starting procedures.
- Get going as soon as you can.
- Control your idling.
- Be an r.p.m. miser.
- Use progressive shifting.
- Maintain efficient engine speed.
- Manage your road speed.
- Operate efficiently in traffic.

For more information, visit www.fleetsmart.gc.ca.

Visible licence plates

By law, your entire licence plate must be completely visible. Remove anything that makes it difficult to see your licence plate, such as dirt, snow, a licence-plate frame or a bike.

If your licence plate is not visible, you may be fined.

Chapter 8-Summary

By the end of this chapter you should know:

- What Ontario's Drive Clean program is and how it works
- What High Occupancy Vehicle (HOV) lanes are and how they work
- Techniques for driving efficiently and saving fuel

CONVERSION CHART

Imperial to Metric Converter

From	To	Multiply By
inches	centimetres	2.54
miles	kilometres	1.61
feet	metres	0.31
pounds	kilograms	0.46
miles per hour	kilometres per hour	1.61

Metric to Imperial Converter

From	To	Multiply By
centimetres	inches	0.39
kilometres	miles	0.62
metres	feet	3.28
kilograms	pounds	2.21
kilometres per hour	miles per hour	0.61

INDEX — THE OFFICIAL MTO BUS HANDBOOK

ONTARIO
BCRE8TVE
YOURS TO DISCOVER

Personalize your licence plates — with two to eight characters, as well as a great choice of colour graphics. Then you'll really stand out from the crowd.

Turn the page to find out more.

NOW THERE ARE MORE WAYS THAN EVER TO EXPRESS YOURSELF!

WE'RE HELPING YOU BUILD CHARACTERS.

Now you've got extra choices when creating your personalized licence plate. We've introduced seven and eight characters. So you've got even more to work with — a minimum of two characters and right up to eight. Just think of the possibilities.

Every personalized plate is one of a kind. No one else can have the same plate as yours.

For more information and to order your personalized plates, call 1-800-AUTO-PL8 (1-800-288-6758).

Or visit the ServiceOntario website: www.serviceontario.ca Or drop by your local ServiceOntario centre.

Gift certificates are available too.

ONTARIO
BCRE8TVE
YOURS TO DISCOVER

ONTARIO
NOWYOURS
YOURS TO DISCOVER

Graphic licence plates are a hit! And now there are more than 40 choices available. Support your favourite Ontario sports team, community or arts organization, professional group or university. Or select a timeless icon like the loon or trillium.

For a totally unique look, add a colour graphic to a personalized plate with up to six characters.

So express yourself — with colour graphics and personalized licence plates.

For more information and to order your plates, call 1-800-AUTO-PL8 (1-800-288-6758).

Or visit our website: www.mto.gov.on.ca
Or drop by your local ServiceOntario centre.

Gift certificates are available too.

ADD SOME COLOUR WHERE IT COUNTS.

OTHER MTO PUBLICATIONS FOR YOU

Copies of this handbook and others may be purchased from a:
- Retail store near you
- DriveTest Centre
- ServiceOntario Centre
- By calling (416) 326-5300 or 1-800-668-9938 (toll free)
- www.serviceontario.ca/publications

Prepayment required by credit card - VISA or Mastercard.
You may also pay with a certified cheque, bank draft or money order at DriveTest Centres.

Handbook and road map prices are subject to applicable H.S.T and shipping handling costs.

THE OFFICIAL DRIVER'S HANDBOOK

THE OFFICIAL MOTORCYCLE HANDBOOK

THE OFFICIAL TRUCK HANDBOOK

THE OFFICIAL BUS HANDBOOK

THE OFFICIAL AIR BRAKE HANDBOOK

THE OFFICIAL ONTARIO ROAD MAP